Identity Theft
Managing Risk of Private Information Online

Adeniyi E. Ola

Safety & Security Key Books

Identity theft

Managing the risk of private information online

A E Ola

Safety and security key books

Identity theft
Managing the risk of private information online

Printed in the USA by CreatSpace (www.createspace.com)

ISBN-13: 978-1975626389
ISBN-10: 1975626389

Safety & Security Key Books
42 Silton Street, Manchester
M9 4NS. UK

Email: niyiola7@gmail.com

Although every effort has been made to ensure that website addresses are correct at time of going to press, the author cannot be held responsible for the content of any website mentioned in this book. It is sometimes possible to find a relocated web page by typing in the address of the home page for a website in the URL window of your browser.

American and British words and symbols equivalents used in this book.

ATM	cash machine
Attorney	Barrister
Certified mail	Recorded delivery
Check	Cheque
Dollar ($)	Pound Sterling (£)
Lawyer	Solicitor
Mailbox	Post box
Officer	Police
Pay envelope	Pay packet
Social security number (SSN)	National Insurance number (NI)
Zip code	Post code

DEDICATION

This book is dedicated to:
All internet users all over the world
Also to:

Omowe

My own wife, Dr (Mrs.) Ibiyemi Ola who taught me how to be gentle

My kids

Who believe in me that I can do anything and always keep me on my toes

Tutor

Stephen Akintayo who pointed out for the umpteenth time, the genius in me

And finally

To those who do not believe in me

You all create the great balance

Table of Contents

Preface

Identity theft, sometimes referred to as identity fraud, is a crime that involves someone using your personal information such as your name, Social Security number, date of birth, credit card number, or other financial account information without your permission to commit fraud and/or other crimes.

Using the advice within these pages, I will show you the steps you can take to reduce and hopefully eliminate any risk to yourself. Your identity and your personal information are valuable.

Criminals can find out your personal details with ease today and use your own details to open bank accounts and get credit cards, loans, state benefits and documents such as passports and driving licenses - all in your name.

The websites listed in the book can help you protect yourself, advises what to do if it happens to you and suggests where to get further help. In the UK alone, the Home Office estimated that identity theft cost the UK £1.3 billion per annum. Experts believe that the real figure could actually be as high as £4.5 billion. Identity theft occurs in many forms, such as someone using your stolen personal information to apply for loans or purchase items using your credit card number, along with many other fraudulent   activities. Because of this, most identity theft victims never incur a high amount of direct monetary losses. However, repairing the damages caused by identity theft can be a lengthy, financially straining process. Taking precautions can therefore save time, money and the stress.

Chapter One
Introduction

How serious is identity theft?

Imagine waking up one morning. You are on your way to an interview for a new job. Maybe you're looking to jump up the corporate ladder or perhaps it's for a second job to help get ahead of the bills. Whatever the case you are optimistic about the day. A friend of yours has given their personal recommendation and you are confident the job is in the bag.

The interview goes well. The interviewer seems pleased with you and you have a good feeling about the offer. While nothing is promised you are more than certain the job is yours as soon as the paperwork is approved.

You finish the interview and stop by the car showroom. It's looking like a good time to finally get that new car you've had your eye on! You've been thinking about it for months. The salesperson takes you for a spin and it's everything you've dreamed of – and more!

Stepping back into the showroom the salesperson suggests you sit down. "Grab a cup of coffee and we'll talk about driving this baby away today!" Sounds good?

Bantering over the paperwork you sit back with a sigh of contentment and put down the pen. "Let's just check your credit and you should be off in a few minutes" he says. Today is a GREAT day!

As you sit back and gaze at the gleaming cars on the showroom floor you notice the salesperson has become rather silent.

"I'm sorry but it looks like this might not work out right now" he says. You look at him and see a sudden sternness in his eyes. "Really," you say "why's that?"

"Well, you've got a few things on your credit report that are a concern. I'm afraid this car would be impossible to finance."

"What do you mean? My credit is fine!" you start to sputter "let me see".

"I'm not allowed to share your report with you, but maybe in a few months you can come back and look again."

You head out the door in confusion. You KNEW you could get that car. What was he talking about?

As you open the door to your home you see the message light flashing on your phone. That was fast! The job offer – that will put you back in a good mood!

"...I'm afraid we won't be able to offer you a position with us right now..." you don't even hear the rest of the message. WHAT??
Ding-dong. The doorbell. Who could that be?
"Hello, I'm Officer Brown, may we have a word with you..."

What identity theft can do to you?

We often take our liberties for granted. What you know life to be can suddenly change if you've been a victim of identity theft.

While you've been busy with your day-to-day life someone could have stolen your personal information and racked up debts or committed fraud – all with your name on it. What happens then can be anything from being denied employment, credit or even being arrested for a crime you didn't commit.

Identity theft is that serious. It is even more serious as it can happen to a dead person!

Victims of identity theft can spend years paying back debts or fighting to restore their credit as well as their reputation. Finding out you are a victim of identity theft can be frightening and a source of anxiety even after you've resolved the issue.

According to a survey conducted in the US by the FTC (Federal Trade and Commission) 4.6% of Americans involved in the survey responded that they had been a victim of identity theft within the past year. That means about 10 million Americans dealt with some form of identity theft – from using existing credit cards to setting up new accounts or giving false identification when arrested for a crime.

It doesn't stop there. The cost of clearing up the theft ranged from an average of $500 to $1200 per victim. It took them on average 30 hours to resolve the issue while also costing time and money for businesses and agencies who assist these victims.

In the UK alone, the Home Office estimated that identity theft cost the UK up to £1.3 billion per annum. Experts believe anyway that the real figure could actually be as high as £4.5 billion in a particular fiscal year.

With all the tools available to potential thieves along with our increasing reliance on paperless money transfers (credit cards, debit cards and online payments) we are incredibly susceptible to having this nightmare come true.

Consider the following cases of identity theft and how it can be used to perpetrate crime:

□□Several people obtained names and Social Security numbers of several hundred high-ranking active-duty and retired U.S. military officers from a public Internet Website. They used the officers' names and numbers to apply for credit cards and bank and corporate credit in the officers' names.

□□A man stole the identities of more than 100 people by working with a woman who had worked in the payroll department of a cellular telephone company. In that position, the woman had access to confidential employee information such as Social Security numbers and home addresses. Using the employees' names and Social Security numbers, the man was able to access their stock trading accounts at an online brokerage and transfer money to another account that he had set up. One victim had more than $287,000 taken from his brokerage account without his knowledge.

When various people who picked up their mail at a U.S. post office threw away merchandise catalogs, which contained identifying information such as their names and account numbers, a woman went through the trash, removed the catalogs, and used the identifying information to order merchandise in other people's names.

A man stole private bank account information about an insurance company's policyholders. He used that information to deposit approximately 4,300 counterfeit bank drafts, totaling more than $764,000, and to withdraw funds from the accounts of the policyholders.

It can happen without you even knowing it, and can ruin lives. It can take a con just a few minutes to ruin a good name you've worked to build.

With the internet, identity theft is going global. The scary part is these criminals are getting better and better. You can become a victim and not even know it was YOU who started the cycle. It can start with a simple e-mail.

The phenomenon has sprung even more non-legitimate scams preying on the fears of having one's identity stolen. People are cashing in on the hysteria and costing consumers even more money.

The victims believe, from experience, that it is the only crime where the suspect is presumed innocent before proven guilty, and the victim is "guilty" until proven "innocent."

In this book, we'll take an in-depth look at identity theft. We'll explore how your personal information can get stolen as well as ways to protect yourself.

This book will tell you the steps you need to take to recover your credit and stop the thieves who stole what you yourself worked to build. We will also have a special section on preventing identity theft through the internet. It's a very real risk you take, but there are ways to keep yourself safe.

Don't let fear of the criminals keep you in a state of suspension. Learn to keep your information safe with our guide to "Protect Yourself from Identity Theft".

What is identity theft?

It's more than a simple impersonation of someone. You've heard of people impersonating a police officer, or the girl who claimed to be Jessica Simpson's personal assistant and securing thousands of dollars of items she used for herself.

Identity theft is a crime that occurs – usually without attaching a face to a name – until the criminal is caught.

Identity theft occurs when your personal information is stolen and used without your knowledge to commit fraud or other crimes. a con artist appropriates another's name, address, Social Security number or other identifying information and uses that information to open new credit card accounts, take over existing accounts, obtain loans in the victim's name or steal funds from the victim's checking, savings, or investment accounts.

"Identity theft" is technically defined as the use, transfer or theft of personal identifying information for the purpose of committing a crime. The U.S. Secret Service defines identity theft as using another person's name and social security number for fraudulent purposes, such as to purchase goods on credit. A larger-scale version is what's called identity takeover, in which thieves use the victim's identity and credit to open bank accounts, apply for credit and even take out loans.

Federal law prevents identity theft victims from being held liable for bills incurred by imposters. Consumers, however, can spend months, and even years, in repairing the damage to their good credit. Businesses are affected greatly as well by this crime. They have given out goods and services with illegally obtained credit cards. With credit protection, as long as the victim can prove they didn't make the purchases, and it is the most difficult thing to do, these businesses must write off the bill without recovering the merchandise.

A similar crime is identity fraud. A variety of abuses of the bankruptcy system, including the concealment of assets in bankruptcy, the making of false sworn financial statements in bankruptcy proceedings, and the filing of bankruptcies under false social security numbers are often dubbed "identity fraud" by prosecutors and government regulators.

Cons attempt to obtain the benefits of bankruptcy such as relief from debt collection, while attempting to escape negative credit consequences.

In one case they leased a residence and obtained credit with the name and social security number of an unsuspecting victim then they occupied the residence, ran up the credit cards, and then filed for bankruptcy in the victim's name. One bankruptcy petition was filed in the name of a recently deceased father.

Such fraudulent bankruptcy filings often wreak havoc on innocent people who must spend substantial resources to clear their credits and their names. The rampant theft and abuse of other people's credit histories and social security numbers has become one of the biggest problems of consumer bankruptcy fraud.

Both crimes have become rampant affecting millions and millions of people in the United States alone. You may think you're protected, but you may be surprised exactly how these criminals get your personal information.

How can you reduce the risk and what do you do if it happens to you or your family?

Chapter Two
Identify the risk

The commercials are all over television – and they certainly are attention-grabbing!

They're the ones where the heavy, bald guy is sitting in his easy chair talking in a squeaky female voice about all the clothes he bought – including a bustier. Or the little old lady speaking with the gruff voice of a younger man about the sweet motorcycle she now owned.

While we might find these commercials funny, the real victims of identity theft find them disturbing and even painful. The media uses these types of ads to alert us to the crime of identity theft and how everyday people can be affected.

You don't have to have a lot of money to be taken advantage of. All you need is a social security number – which, of course, we all have.

The criminals who perpetrate the crime of identity theft are sly and cunning. Before you can even know it, your credit is ruined and you must "jump through hoops" just to get it repaired a small bit.

Identity theft is a serious crime – one that is occurring with an alarming frequency.

If you think you've figured out how to keep the thieves out of your personal information you may be surprised at the methods they use to gain access to it. Finding out HOW thieves access your information is the first step in reducing the risk.

How they get your information?

Lost or stolen wallet

A lost or stolen wallet is just one way for a thief to get your information.

They can then fraudulently access your credit report by posing as an employer, loan officer, or landlord.

Not surprisingly a person who has had their wallet lost or stolen is at great risk of becoming a victim of identity theft. Carrying important documents like your Social Security Number or National Insurance Number, birth certificate, driver's license and credit or debit cards in your wallet can give a thief easy access to your personal information.

Missing mail

If you think you've missed a couple bills or know that your mail box has been broken into, your personal information may have been stolen. Credit card bills, offers for credit cards and information that contains personal information or your SSN/NI can be used to gain access to unauthorized credit or to commit fraud in your name.

Garbage

Thinking of throwing the latest credit card offer in the garbage? Clearing out old tax forms or other personal information? Rummaging through the garbage for such information is known as 'dumpster diving' and can be an easy source for identity thieves. Your personal garbage isn't the only source – businesses that collect personal information can also be targeted.

Criminals will therefore go dumpster diving looking for bills or other papers with your personal information on it. Many people receive daily offers for credit cards. If you're not interested, you just throw it away. Thieves love finding these! The problem of criminals rummaging through bins for such documents is well known and there have even been reports of organized gangs paying people to pick through landfill sites for such documents.

'Phishing' or 'pretexting'

By far the biggest problem with identity theft is 'social engineering': this means someone obtaining information by deception, and usually involves some form of incentive or plain old-fashioned flattery. A veneer of officialdom also oils the wheels and it's a surprisingly effective technique.

Several recent experiments have shown that nine in 10 people would give up computer passwords in exchange for a small gift like a chocolate bar when questioned by someone holding a clipboard. All too frequently people give out sensitive information over the telephone when they have no proof that the person at the other end is who they say they are.

While identity theft committed in this manner still accounts for the majority of fraud, security experts are warning that such attacks are increasingly being abandoned in favor of electronic methods.

One of the most dangerous methods of identity theft used online is key logging, which bypasses documents altogether. Here a piece of software records every keystroke made on the computer, including all of your log-in details. Such software is generally spread by viruses or as attachments in spam.

Email in particular allows personal contact with millions of people at the push of a button and fraudsters have taken advantage of this. It has also allowed for the merging of old and new types of identity theft to create potentially devastating crimes such as phishing.

This is another old con in modern form and involves setting up a plausible looking website that claims to be an online business. It's a cheaper, more anonymous variant of fly-by-night operators setting up stalls in abandoned shops.

Visitors are encouraged to input personal information, usually after receiving an email requesting they confirm log-in details or check the status of an order. Such emails are sent out to millions of addresses and usually contain warnings that action must be taken immediately in order to frighten the recipient into acting without thinking.

This is an especially scary way of obtaining your information since most of these e-mails are very, very real looking. The non-educated consumer can easily be taken in by simply clicking on a link and entering in a password.

This is especially common for people who have Pay Pal accounts or who sell at online auction sites like eBay.

Web monitoring and hosting companies work hard to shut these websites down within days but they can harvest thousands of account details in that time.

Pretexting, also known in the UK as *blagging* or *bohoing*, is the act of creating and using an invented scenario (the pretext) to engage a targeted victim in a manner that increases the chance the victim will divulge information or perform actions that would be unlikely in ordinary circumstances.

Online or over the phone there are unscrupulous individuals masquerading as legitimate businesses in an attempt to convince you to pass on personal information for illegal purposes? Any requests to 'validate account information' by providing personal information online or over the phone should be questioned.

Businesses or employees

Employees or businesses that have legitimate access to your personal information may use that information for non-business activities. Identity thieves that work in institutions that contain sensitive personal data may abuse the access they have or even present themselves to you as someone that should have access, such as a landlord or employer.

'Skimming'

Shoulder surfing is done at the ATM machine and phone booths. This means the criminal will stand behind you as you enter in your PIN number or phone information.

Police have already arrested several individuals copying cards using the cash machines themselves. A small electronic camera is mounted above the keypad of the cash machine and a card reader, often only a few centimeters thick, goes over the card slot.

At a busy machine hundreds of card numbers can be collected in a few hours and turned into cloned cards. The wide availability of small card scanners has also made card skimming a problem. In a matter of seconds your card's magnetic strip can be copied and a crooked employee of a restaurant or retail outlet can copy many cards in a day.

Thieves have access to all these 'tools of the trade' that allow them to steal information from your card at ATMs or during a card swipe for a purchase. These data storing devices capture your information without your realizing it.

Change of address

A change of address form can be used to divert billing statements to another location. This will give them access to your credit card numbers.

By filling out a form at the post office the identity thief can have your bills and other personal mail diverted to a new address. It may take you a few days to realize what has happened and make the correction. Post Offices in many countries normally write to inform addresses of an intention to redirect letters to another address. If you happen to find such a letter, it will pay dividends to contact the post office right away.

Spyware

A new threat on the scene is from computer viruses that 'spy' on you while you shop or do banking online. Any website that you enter personal information into can be 'spied on' putting you at risk. Online banks in particular have been targeted but so too have eBay and PayPal.

An even more advanced, and harder to detect, form of this con has come to light recently nicknamed pharming. This involves criminals using computer security holes to reprogram computers that allocate the addresses for all web pages so even if you key in the correct web address, your web browser may be directed to a bogus site. Such attacks are technically possible although none have been confirmed as yet.

Unsecured online transactions
Online shopping at a site that is not secured can potentially put you at risk of having your information stolen. Websites may also collect and sell some of your information without your knowledge unless their posted Privacy Policy states otherwise.

Break in
Anytime you or a business that has your information is a victim of a break in you may have had personal information stolen.

Personal Computers
Are you storing sensitive passwords on your laptop? Are you throwing out an old computer? If your laptop is stolen or accessed by a thief they may be able to find that information. Old computers may hold information on their hard drives even when you've deleted it.

There are many more ways criminals can access your personal information. How can you find out if you have become a victim?

How do you know if your identity's been stolen?

If you know that your personal information has been accessed or otherwise tampered with there are steps you must take to stop the thieves and try to repair the damage. It is important to stay alert to signs that your information is being used without your consent even when you don't suspect you've been a victim.

Staying alert to these signs will help you respond quickly if your identity has been stolen:

☐ Unfamiliar charges or withdrawals
Always check your bank and credit card statements and make immediate inquiries to unfamiliar charges and withdrawals.

☐ Missing mail
If your bills and other mail have gone missing a thief may have broken into your mail box or had your mail redirected to a new address.

☐ Calls from Creditors
If you are being contacted by creditors you did not do business with you need to take immediate action to find out who has?

☐ New Credit Cards
Receiving new credit cards or bills that you didn't sign for is a danger sign that your identity may have been stolen.

☐ Denial of Credit
Unexplained refusal of credit requires investigation on your part. You need to get access to your credit report right away.

What to do if you are a victim of identity theft

Unfortunately, the most common way people find out they are victims of identity theft is when the damage is already done.

One victim tells the account of how she found out her information had been stolen. She writes:

"I had been thinking about buying a cellular phone but someone beat me to the punch. This person set up an account using his name and paid two bills using my Visa/debit card number. I'm not sure how he got the number since there's only one card. I've heard a lot of theories in the last few days.

Nextel allowed this man to set up the account using my card and never verified the information. Had they checked him out, they might have found that the owner of the Visa/debit card was a woman, and not the man starting a cellular phone account. I don't even have a cell phone! The guy took more than half my paycheck, leaving me home all weekend with very little money. Luckily, rent wasn't due."

Yet another victim writes:

"On Xxxx xx, 2016 - my birthday - my wallet was taken at the checkout counter at (a grocery store). Security cameras showed the checker taking my wallet, and charging nearly $500 of groceries after I left the store.

Despite my calling the police, no charges were filed against the individual because he not "steal" the wallet from my person.

The wallet -containing my recently renewed Driver's License, MasterCard, ATM Card, parking card, business cards (with cellular and home numbers), and college ID card (with social security number on it) – was never recovered. The head of store security and the police detective told me that the wallet was probably thrown away."

And a third account of identity theft reads:

"On September 19, I first became aware that my identity had been stolen. I received a bill from (a department store) - for $675.55 of electronic purchases I did not make. I notified (them), and put fraud alerts at the three credit reporting agencies, and ordered copies of my credit reports.

I was dumbfounded by what I discovered: over $7,000 of charges on seven credit cards, with attempts to open 6 more. Starting on September 9th, most accounts had been opened on the Internet. Despite the fraud alert, accounts are still being opened. An account was opened at (a furniture store) on September 22nd.

The suspect presented my driver's license - and, despite the fraud alert, the miswriting of my social security number, and obvious differences in the signature - was granted instant credit. Subsequently, nearly $3000 in charges were made, in 6 separate instances, over a four-day period."

By the time these people discovered their identity had been stolen, their credit had already been jeopardized and perhaps even ruined. They would have to embark on the unfortunate and long journey of proving their innocence.

Though we have touched on it in this book, one thing you can do is to monitor your credit reports faithfully, in fact religiously. You should also be aware when bills do not arrive as expected or you receive statements for credit cards that you do not have.

You may be denied credit for a large purchase and not be given an immediate reason why. This is a HUGE warning sign that your identity may have been compromised – especially if you've always had an excellent credit score.

Finally, if you are receiving phone calls or correspondence from credit reporting agencies or collection departments, you need to look at your credit more closely to see if your information has been breached.

These are all warning signs that you should not ignore – under any circumstances!

If the worst has happened and you find out you have indeed been a victim of identity theft (or have reason to suspect it) you must take IMMEDIATE action to control the damage. So what do you do if you think you're a victim of identity theft? The first thing you'll need to do is gather important documents and be able to prove your identity.

Chapter Three
Proof of identity

How do I prove my identity?

You might think this would be the easiest part of combating identity theft, but it really isn't. Think about it. The thief was allowed to pose as you, how do the companies know that you're not also just trying to impersonate someone else?

Applications or other transaction records related to the theft of your identity may help you prove that you are a victim. For example, you may be able to show that the signature on an application is not yours.

These documents also may contain information about the identity thief that is valuable to law enforcement. By law, companies must give you a copy of the application or other business transaction records relating to your identity theft if you submit your request in writing.

Be sure to ask the company representative where you should mail your request. Companies must provide these records at no charge to you within 30 days of receipt of your request and supporting documents. You also may give permission to any law enforcement agency to get these records, or ask in your written request that a copy of these records be sent to a particular law enforcement officer.

The company can ask you for proof of your identity. This may be a photocopy of a government-issued ID card, the same type of information the identity thief used to open or access the account, or the type of information the company usually requests from applicants or customers, and a police report and a completed affidavit, which may be an Identity Theft Affidavit or the company's own affidavit.

This all, of course, is a daunting process. There are steps you can take, however, to organize your case and have all the documents you need at hand to combat the theft of your identity.

Organizing your case

Accurate and complete records will help you to resolve your identity theft case more quickly.

Have a plan when you contact a company. Don't assume that the person you talk to will give you all the information or help you need. Prepare a list of questions to ask the representative, as well as information about your identity theft.

Don't end the call until you're sure you understand everything you've been told. If you need more help, ask to speak to a supervisor.

Write down the name of everyone you talk to, what he or she tells you, and the date the conversation occurred. At the end of the book, we'll provide you with a form to plan out your course of action. Follow this course to provide the most accurate and up-to-date information you can.

Follow up in writing with all contacts you've made on the phone or in person. Use certified mail, return receipt requested, or recorded delivery so you can document what the company or organization received and when. Keep copies of all correspondence or forms you send. Keep the originals of supporting documents, like police reports and letters to and from creditors; send copies only.

Set up a filing system for easy access to your paperwork. Keep old files even if you believe your case is closed. Once resolved, most cases stay resolved, but problems can crop up.

At this point, you can start the tedious task of contacting the companies you need to in order to get the problem cleared up.

What to do first

What to do first depends on where you have been hit most. Is it through banking transaction, credit card fraud or online shopping? If you have become a victim of identity theft, you are going to be embarking on a long and perilous journey that will, no doubt, be extremely frustrating and filled with stress.

Unless you want to accept responsibility for what the thieves did to you – and we assume you don't – accepting the fact that this will take some time to unravel is your very first step. You will be talking to a lot of people, copying a lot of documents, and gathering a lot of information. Patience is key here, so keep that in mind.

The first thing to do is contact your bank or financial institution and put them on notice that your personal information has been compromised. You must also contact credit card companies.

Close accounts, like credit cards and bank accounts, immediately. When you open new accounts place passwords on them. Avoid using your mother's maiden name, your birth date, and the last four digits of your Social Security Number (SSN) or your phone number, or a series of consecutive numbers.

Call and speak with someone in the security or fraud department of each company. Follow up in writing, and include copies (NOT originals) of supporting documents. It's important to notify credit card companies and banks in writing.

Send your letters by certified mail, return receipt requested, or recorded delivery so you can document what the company received and when. Keep a file of your correspondence and enclosures.

When you open new accounts, use new Personal Identification Numbers (PINs) and passwords. As we've said, avoid using easily available information like your mother's maiden name, your birth date, the last four digits of your SSN or your phone number, or a series of consecutive numbers. This is extremely important, so it bears repeating.

If the identity thief has made charges or debits on your accounts, or on fraudulently opened accounts, ask the company for the forms to dispute those transactions:

☐☐For charges and debits on existing accounts, ask the representative to send you the company's fraud dispute forms. If the company doesn't have special forms, write a letter to dispute the fraudulent charges or debits. In either case, write to the company at the address given for "billing inquiries," NOT the address for sending your payments.

☐☐For new unauthorized accounts, ask the representative to send you the company's fraud dispute forms. If the company already has reported these accounts or debts on your credit report, dispute this fraudulent information.

Once you have resolved your identity theft dispute with the company, ask for a letter stating that the company has closed the disputed accounts and has discharged the fraudulent debts. This letter is your best proof if errors relating to this account reappear on your credit report or you are contacted again about the fraudulent debt.

Report to the Credit Bureaus

If you are a victim of identity theft you must report it immediately to one of the three major credit bureaus. Call the toll-free fraud number of any of the three nationwide consumer reporting companies and place an initial fraud alert on your credit reports. An alert can help stop someone from opening new credit accounts in your name. We have the contact information for the three credit reporting agencies at the end of the book.

You only need to call one bureau to place the fraud alert and they will forward the information to the other two. Your SSN will be flagged for 90 days to prevent a thief from trying to obtain new credit with your identification.

A note about fraud alerts needs to be inserted here. There are two types of fraud alerts: an initial alert, and an extended alert.

□□An initial alert stays on your credit report for at least 90 days. You may ask that an initial fraud alert be placed on your credit report if you suspect you have been, or are about to be, a victim of identity theft. An initial alert is appropriate if your wallet has been stolen or if you've been taken in by a "phishing" scam. When you place an initial fraud alert on your credit report, you're entitled to one free credit report from each of the three nationwide consumer reporting companies.

□□ If you are certain that your identity has been stolen you can request an extended fraud alert. The extended fraud alert will remain on your report for seven years and will require you to submit an identity theft police report. You can have an extended alert placed on your credit report if you've been a victim of identity theft and you provide the consumer reporting company with an "identity theft report."

When you place an extended alert on your credit report, you're entitled to two free credit reports within twelve months from each of the three nationwide consumer reporting companies. In addition, the consumer reporting companies will remove your name from marketing lists for prescreened credit offers for five years unless you ask them to put your name back on the list before then.

To place either of these alerts on your credit report, or to have them removed, you will be required to provide appropriate proof of your identity: that may include your SSN, name, address and other personal information requested by the consumer reporting company.

When a business sees the alert on your credit report, they must verify your identity before issuing you credit. As part of this verification process, the business may try to contact you directly. This may cause some delays if you're trying to obtain credit. To compensate for possible delays, you may wish to include a cell phone number, where you can be reached easily, in your alert. Remember to keep all contact information in your alert current.

Once you place the fraud alert in your file, you're entitled to order free copies of your credit reports, and, if you ask, only the last four digits of your SSN will appear on your credit reports. Once you get your credit reports, review them carefully.

Look for inquiries from companies you haven't contacted, accounts you didn't open, and debts on your accounts that you can't explain. Check that information, like your SSN, address, name or initials, and employers are correct. If you find fraudulent or inaccurate information, get it removed.

Continue to check your credit reports periodically, especially for the first year after you discover the identity theft, to make sure no new fraudulent activity has occurred.

Flagging your account will alert potential creditors to take steps to protect you. This will also delay the credit approval process.

The three bureaus in the US are below: credit agencies in other countries are also given later in the book:

- Equifax: 1-800-525-6285

www.equifax.com P.O. Box 740241, Atlanta, GA 30374-0241

- TransUnion: 1-800-680-7289

www.transunion.com Fraud Victim Assistance Division, P.O. Box 6790, Fullerton, CA 92834-6790

- Experian: 1-888-EXPERIAN (397-3742)

www.experian.com P.O. Box 9532, Allen, TX 75013

You will be asked for your SSN and other identifying information through an automated service. The alert will be passed on to the other two bureaus and all three credit bureaus will send you a letter to confirm the fraud alert is in place. You will also be given directions for obtaining your credit report for free from each of the bureaus.

The credit reports will have a telephone number listed on them if you need to contact the bureaus about fraudulent activity listed on the reports.

Get Copies of Your Credit Report
Send for your credit reports following the instructions from the credit bureaus. Review the reports carefully. Look for creditor's names that you did not request credit from. Also check your personal information; SSN, address, name, initials and employer information.
Order your credit report at least every three months for the first year of the fraud. Some areas provide a free report every 12 months. Other areas will give you several free reports for the year you report an identity theft. Some will charge for each report. Tell them you are an identity theft victim and ask for a free report. A number of credit reference agencies allow you to have regular online access to your credit report when you register with them for a token. Each change in your credit situation are recorded and you could print out your report at will.

File a police report
Keep records of the fraudulent activity as proof for your report. Blackout unrelated activity and give copies to the police. Give them any new evidence as it turns up and keep a copy of the report as proof for creditors and the credit bureaus.

Collect account information
Contact the creditors who issued accounts to the identity thief. The Police may give you a form to request the information. Send a copy of the

police report and the account statements to the creditor. Pass any new information over to the police.

Close the accounts

For NEW Accounts created by the thief: Call the creditors (including credit cards, department stores and cell phone accounts) and ask for their security or fraud department. Tell them you are an identity theft victim and ask them to close the accounts and report the closing to the credit bureau. If the account has already been used by the thief ask them not to hold you responsible for the debt.

For EXISTING Accounts used fraudulently by a thief, Close the accounts and ask the creditors to report the closing to the credit bureaus. Request that they declare the account "closed at consumer's request". If you open a new account don't use personal information like your mother's maiden name or your SSN for a password. If those are the only options request to use a different password.

Alert government agencies

If your BRP, SSN, NI, driver's license or other government ID has been stolen report it to the proper agency to cancel it and order a replacement. Ask that your information be flagged so that no one else can get copies. When it comes to your driver's license, contact DVLA, the agency that issued the license or other identification document. Follow its procedures to cancel the document and to get a replacement. Ask the agency to flag your file so that no one else can get a license or any other identification document from them in your name.

If your information has been misused, file a report about the theft with the police, and file a complaint with the Federal Trade Commission, as well. If another crime was committed for example, if your purse or wallet was stolen or your house or car was broken into report it to the police immediately.

In all cases of identity theft or fraud, you will be doubly covered by reporting it to the police. They will take a report documenting the crime.

After you file the police report, get a copy of it or at the very least, the number of the report. It can help you deal with creditors who need proof of the crime.

If the police are reluctant to take your report, ask to file a "Miscellaneous Incidents" report, or try another jurisdiction, like your state police. You also can check with your state Attorney General's office to find out if state law requires the police to take reports for identity theft. Check the Blue Pages of your telephone directory for the phone number or check www.naag.org for a list of state Attorneys General.

As far as the FTC is concerned, by sharing your identity theft complaint with the FTC, you will provide important information that can help law enforcement officials across the nation track down identity thieves and stop them. The FTC can refer victims' complaints to other government agencies and companies for further action, as well as investigate companies for violations of laws the agency enforces.

You can file a complaint online at www.consumer.gov/idtheft. If you don't have Internet access, call the FTC's Identity Theft Hotline, toll-free: 1-877- IDTHEFT (438-4338); TTY: 1-866-653- 4261; or write: Identity Theft Clearinghouse, Federal Trade Commission, 600 Pennsylvania Avenue, NW, Washington, DC 20580.

Be sure to call the Hotline to update your complaint if you have any additional information or problems.

Once you've made these initial steps, there are some specific things that must be done with specific situations.

Chapter Four
Correcting Id errors

Resolving specific problems

Because the thief has gained access to your personal information, it's a good idea to protect everything that has to do with your financial information.

Some of this information has been touched on previously, but it all bears repeating.

Bank accounts and electronic withdrawals

Different laws determine your legal remedies based on the type of bank fraud you have suffered. For example, in the US, state laws protect you against fraud committed by a thief using paper documents, like stolen or counterfeit checks.

But if the thief used an electronic fund transfer, federal law applies. Many transactions may seem to be processed electronically but are still considered "paper" transactions. If you're not sure what type of transaction the thief used to commit the fraud, ask the financial institution that processed the transaction.

The Electronic Fund Transfer Act provides consumer protections for transactions involving an ATM or debit card, or another electronic way to debit or credit an account. It also limits your liability for unauthorized electronic fund transfers.

You have 60 days from the date your bank account statement is sent to you to report in writing any money withdrawn from your account without your permission. This includes instances when your credit or debit card is "skimmed" that is, when a thief captures your account number and PIN without your card having been lost or stolen.

If your ATM or debit card is lost or stolen, report it immediately because the amount you can be held responsible for depends on how quickly you report the loss.

If you report the loss within two business days of discovery, your personal loss is limited to $50. If you report the loss or theft after two business days, but within 60 days after the unauthorized electronic fund transfer appears on your statement, you could lose up to $500 of what the thief withdraws. If you wait more than 60 days to report the loss or theft, you could lose all the money that was taken from your account after the end of the 60 days.

VISA and MasterCard have voluntarily agreed to limit consumers' liability for unauthorized use of their debit cards in most instances to $50 per card, no matter how much time has elapsed since the discovery of the loss or theft of the card.

The best way to protect yourself in the event of an error or fraudulent transaction is to call the financial institution and follow up in writing by certified letter, return receipt requested so you can prove when the institution received your letter. Keep a copy of the letter you send for your records.

After receiving your notification about an error on your statement, the institution generally has 10 business days to investigate. The institution must tell you the results of its investigation within three business days after completing it and must correct an error within one business day after determining that it occurred.

If the institution needs more time, it may take up to 45 days to complete the investigation but only if the money in dispute is returned to your account and you are notified promptly of the credit. At the end of the investigation, if no error has been found, the institution may take the money back if it sends you a written explanation.

In general, if an identity thief steals your checks or counterfeits checks from your existing bank account, stop payment, close the account, and ask your bank to notify Chex Systems, Inc. or the check verification service with which it does business. That way, retailers can be notified not to accept these checks.

While no federal law limits your losses if someone uses your checks with a forged signature, or uses another type of "paper" transaction such as a demand draft, state laws may protect you. Most states hold the bank responsible for losses from such transactions.

At the same time, most states require you to take reasonable care of your account. For example, you may be held responsible for the forgery if you fail to notify the bank in a timely manner that a check was lost or stolen. Contact your state banking or consumer protection agency for more information.

You can contact major check verification companies directly.

To request that they notify retailers who use their databases not to accept your checks, call: TeleCheck at 1-800-710-9898 or 1-800-927-0188

Certegy, Inc. (previously Equifax Check Systems) at 1-800-437-5120

To find out if the identity thief has been passing bad checks in your name, call:

SCAN: 1-800-262-7771

If your checks are rejected by a merchant, it may be because an identity thief is using the Magnetic Information Character Recognition (MICR) code (the numbers at the bottom of checks), your driver's license number, or another identification number.

The merchant who rejects your check should give you its check verification company contact information so you can find out what information the thief is using. If you find that the thief is using your MICR code, ask your bank to close your checking account, and open a new one.

If you discover that the thief is using your driver's license number or some other identification number, work with your DMV or other identification issuing agency to get new identification with new numbers.

Once you have taken the appropriate steps, your checks should be accepted.

The check verification company may or may not remove the information about the MICR code or the driver's license/identification number from its database because this information may help prevent the thief from continuing to commit fraud.

If the checks are being passed on a new account, contact the bank to close the account. Also contact Chex Systems, Inc., to review your consumer report to make sure that no other bank accounts have been opened in your name. Dispute any bad checks passed in your name with merchants so they don't start any collections actions against you.

Fraudulent new accounts

If you have trouble opening a new checking account, it may be because an identity thief has been opening accounts in your name. Chex Systems, Inc., produces consumer reports specifically about checking accounts, and as a consumer reporting company, is subject to the Fair Credit Reporting Act.

You can request a free copy of your consumer report by contacting Chex
Systems, Inc. If you find inaccurate information on your consumer report, follow the procedures under Correcting Credit Reports to dispute it.

Contact each of the banks where account inquiries were made, too. This will help ensure that any fraudulently opened accounts are closed.

Chex Systems, Inc.: 1-800-428-9623;
Fax: 602-659-2197
Chex Systems, Inc.
Attn: Consumer Relations
7805 Hudson Road, Suite 100
Woodbury, MN 55125
www.chexhelp.com

Bankruptcy fraud

If you believe someone has filed for bankruptcy in your name, write to the
U.S. Trustee in the region where the bankruptcy was filed. A list of the United State Trustee Programs Regional Offices is available on the UST website. You can as well check the Blue Pages of your phone book under U.S. Government Bankruptcy Administration.

In your letter, describe the situation and provide proof of your identity. The U.S. Trustee will make a criminal referral to law enforcement authorities if you provide appropriate documentation to substantiate your claim.

You also may want to file a complaint with the U.S. Attorney and/or the FBI in the city where the bankruptcy was filed. The U.S. Trustee does not provide legal representation, legal advice, or referrals to lawyers. That means you may need to hire an attorney to help convince the bankruptcy court that the filing is fraudulent. The U.S. Trustee does not provide consumers with copies of court documents. You can get them from the bankruptcy clerk's office for a fee.

Credit cards

The Fair Credit Billing Act establishes procedures for resolving billing errors on your credit card accounts, including fraudulent charges on your accounts. The law also limits your liability for unauthorized credit card charges to $50 per card. To take advantage of the law's consumer protections, you must:

☐☐ Write to the creditor at the address given for "billing inquiries," NOT the address for sending your payments. Include your name, address, account number, and a description of the billing error, including the amount and date of the error. See Sample Letter.

☐☐ Send your letter so that it reaches the creditor within 60 days after the first bill containing the error was mailed to you. If an identity thief changed the address on your account and you didn't receive the bill, your dispute letter still must reach the creditor within 60 days of when the creditor would have mailed the bill. This is one reason it's essential to keep track of your billing statements, and follow up quickly if your bills don't arrive on time. You should send your letter by certified mail, and request a return receipt. It becomes your proof of the date the creditor received the letter. Include copies (NOT originals) of your police report or other documents that support your position. Keep a copy of your dispute letter. The creditor must acknowledge your complaint in writing within 30 days after receiving it, unless the problem has been resolved. The creditor must resolve the dispute within two billing cycles (but not more than 90 days) after receiving your letter.

Complete an identity theft affidavit

In order to remove the debts created by the identity thief you will need to send an affidavit to the company or creditor holding the debt. When you contact them to close the accounts ask what forms they require. The affidavit permits them to investigate the claim – it does not ensure that the debt will be cleared.

While each business may have its own requirements you can also obtain a free affidavit form at: http://www.ftc.gov/bcp/conline/pubs/credit/affidavit.pdf. Ask the business if they will accept this form or need you to fill out one of theirs.

Send the copies of the affidavit and supporting documents to the businesses (a separate form should be created for each account or institution responsible for providing the identity thief with credit). Do not send original bank or card statements. Blackout any information on the statements not related to the account.

Send a copy of each affidavit and the police report to the credit bureaus. Write a letter requesting the information you declared was a result of theft be blocked or removed from your credit report.

Criminal violations

Procedures to correct your record within criminal justice databases can vary from state to state, and even from county to county. Some states have enacted laws with special procedures for identity theft victims to follow to clear their names. You should check with the office of your state Attorney General, but you can use the following information as a general guide.

If wrongful criminal violations are attributed to your name, contact the police or sheriff's department that originally arrested the person using your identity, or the court agency that issued the warrant for the arrest. File an impersonation report with the police/sheriff's department or the court, and confirm your identity.

Ask the police department to take a full set of your fingerprints, photograph you, and make copies of your photo identification documents, like your driver's license, passport, or travel visa. To establish your innocence, ask the police to compare the prints and photographs with those of the imposter.

If the arrest warrant is from a state or county other than where you live, ask your local police department to send the impersonation report to the police department in the jurisdiction where the arrest warrant, traffic citation, or criminal conviction originated.

The law enforcement agency should then recall any warrants and issue a "clearance letter" or "certificate of release" (if the thief was arrested or booked).

You'll need to keep this document with you at all times in case you're wrongly arrested again.

Ask the law enforcement agency to file the record of the follow-up investigation establishing your innocence with the district attorney's (D.A.) office and/or court where the crime took place. This will result in an amended complaint.

Once your name is recorded in a criminal database, it's unlikely that it will be completely removed from the official record. Ask that the "key name" or "primary name" be changed from your name to the imposter's name (or to "John Doe" if the imposter's true identity is not known), with your name noted as an alias. You'll also want to clear your name in the court records. To do this you'll need to determine which state law(s) will help you with this and how. If your state has no formal procedure for clearing your record, contact the D.A.'s office in the county where the case was originally prosecuted. Ask the D.A.'s office for the appropriate court records needed to clear your name. You may need to hire a criminal defense attorney to help you clear your name. You can contact Legal Services in your state or your local bar association for help in finding an attorney.

Finally, contact your state Department of Motor Vehicles (DMV/DVLA) to find out if your driver's license is being used by the identity thief. Ask that your files be flagged for possible fraud.

Stopping debt collectors

The Fair Debt Collection Practices Act prohibits debt collectors from using unfair or deceptive practices to collect overdue bills that a creditor has forwarded for collection, even if those bills don't result from identity theft.

You can stop a debt collector from contacting you in two ways:

☐☐ Write a letter to the collection agency telling them to stop. Once the debt collector receives your letter, the company may not contact you again with two exceptions: They can tell you there will be no further contact, and they can tell you that the debt collector or the creditor intends to take some specific action.

☐☐ Send a letter to the collection agency, within 30 days after you received written notice of the debt, telling them that you do not owe the money.

Include copies of documents that support your position. Including a copy (NOT original) of your police report may be useful. In this case, a collector can renew collection activities only if it sends you proof of the debt. If you don't have documentation to support your position, be as specific as possible about why the debt collector is mistaken. The debt collector is responsible for sending you proof that you're wrong. For example, if the debt you're disputing originates from a credit card you never applied for; ask for a copy of the application with the applicant's signature. Then, you can prove that it's not your signature. If you tell the debt collector that you are a victim of identity theft and it is collecting the debt for another company, the debt collector must tell that company that you may be a victim of identity theft. While you can stop a debt collector from contacting you, that won't get rid of the debt itself. It's important to contact the company that originally opened the account to dispute the debt, otherwise that company may send it to a different debt collector, report it on your credit report, or initiate a lawsuit to collect on the debt.

Phone fraud

If an identity thief has established phone service in your name, is making unauthorized calls that seem to come from and are billed to your cellular phone, or is using your calling card and PIN, contact your service provider immediately to cancel the account and/or calling card.

Open new accounts and choose new PIN numbers. Most companies will work with you to remove the fraudulent charges. If you're having trouble getting them removed from your account or getting an unauthorized account closed, contact the Federal Communications Commission. We have listed their contact info in the section under important numbers. You will, of course, also need to begin having your credit report corrected.

Report stolen mail

If you believe that your mail has been stolen you must contact the nearest Postal Inspector. You can look for the number in your white pages under Government Services, call 1-800-ASK-USPS or search online at http://www.usps.com/ncsc/locators/find-is.html. The USPIS is the law enforcement arm of the U.S. Postal Service, and investigates cases of identity theft. The USPIS has primary jurisdiction in all matters infringing on the integrity of the U.S. mail. If an identity thief has stolen your mail to get new credit cards, bank or credit card statements, pre-screened credit offers, or tax information, or has falsified change-of-address forms or obtained your personal information through a fraud conducted by mail, report it to your local postal inspector. You will then want to get a post office box instead of having local delivery to protect your mail.

Chapter Five
Credit information

Correcting your credit report

Your credit report contains information about where you live, how you pay your bills, and whether you've been sued, arrested, or filed for bankruptcy. Consumer reporting companies sell the information in your report to creditors, insurers, employers, and other businesses that use it to evaluate your applications for credit, insurance, employment, or renting a home. The federal Fair Credit Reporting Act (FCRA) promotes the accuracy and privacy of information in the files of the nation's consumer reporting companies. In the case of identity theft and/or fraud, this step is essential in regaining your identity. Under the FCRA, both the consumer reporting company and the information provider (that is, the person, company, or organization that provides information about you to a consumer reporting company) are responsible for correcting inaccurate or incomplete information in your report. To take advantage of all your rights under this law, contact the consumer reporting company and the information provider.

Tell the consumer reporting company, in writing, what information you think is inaccurate. Include copies (NOT originals) of documents that support your position. This would include a copy of the police report you have filed.

In addition to providing your complete name and address, your letter should clearly identify each item in your report you dispute, state the facts and explain why you dispute the information, and request that it be removed or corrected. You may want to enclose a copy of your report with the items in question circled. Send your letter by certified mail, "return receipt requested," so you can document what the consumer reporting company received. Keep copies of your dispute letter and enclosures.

Consumer reporting companies must investigate the items in question— usually within 30 days— unless they consider your dispute frivolous. They also must forward all the relevant data you provide about the inaccuracy to the organization that provided the information. After the information provider receives notice of a dispute from the consumer reporting company, it must investigate, review the relevant information, and report the results back to the consumer reporting company. If the information provider finds the disputed information is inaccurate, it must notify all three nationwide consumer reporting companies so they can correct the information in your file. When the investigation is complete, the consumer reporting company must give you the results in writing and a free copy of your report if the dispute results in a change. This free report does not count as your annual free report.

If an item is changed or deleted, the consumer reporting company cannot put the disputed information back in your file unless the information provider verifies that it is accurate and complete. The consumer reporting company also must send you written notice that includes the name, address, and phone number of the information provider.

If you ask, the consumer reporting company must send notices of any corrections to anyone who received your report in the past six months. You can have a corrected copy of your report sent to anyone who received a copy during the past two years for employment purposes.

If an investigation doesn't resolve your dispute with the consumer reporting company, you can ask that a statement of the dispute be included in your file and in future reports. You also can ask the consumer reporting company to provide your statement to anyone who received a copy of your report in the recent past. You can expect to pay a fee for this service.

You should also tell the creditor or other information provider, in writing, that you dispute an item. Be sure to include copies (NOT originals) of documents that support your position. Many providers specify an address for disputes.

If the provider reports the item to a consumer reporting company, it must include a notice of your dispute. And if you are correct—that is, if the information is found to be inaccurate—the information provider may not report it again.

While the most information above is provided for those living in the US the steps are nearly the same in other countries. Here are some links and numbers to credit and police agencies in the UK, Canada and Australia.

Contact Numbers for the UK

If you are a victim of identity theft in the UK use the following contact information:

Credit Bureaus

☐ Call Credit: 44 (0) 113 244 1555
www.callcredit.co.uk/
Callcredit plc, One Park Lane, Leeds.
West Yorkshire, LS3 1EP.

☐ Equifax: 0870 010 2091 for the CIFAS Protective Registration Service
www.equifax.co.uk/
Credit File Advice Centre PO Box 1140,
Bradford, BD1 5US

☐ Experian: 0870 241 6212 (M-F 8-6, Sat 9-1)
www.experian.co.uk/ Experian Ltd,
PO Box 9000,
Nottingham, NG80 7WP

Police
File a report at your local Police Station. Locate the closest station at http://police.uk.

Contact Numbers for Canada

If you are a victim of identity theft in Canada use the following contact information;

Credit Bureaus
☐   Trans Union Canada:
1-877-525-3823 (Quebec Residents: 1-877-713-3393)
www.tuc.ca

☐   Equifax Canada:
1-800-465-7166 www.equifax.ca
Equifax Canada Inc. Consumer Relations Department,
Box 190 Jean Talon Station,
Montreal, Quebec,
H1S 2Z2

Hotline
PhoneBusters National Call Centre – with a mandate to gather information and intelligence about identity theft PhoneBusters will provide advice and assistance. Toll free at 1-888-495-8501

If you are a victim of identity theft in Australia use the following contact information;

Credit Bureaus

☐   Baycorp Advantage: (02) 9464 6000
www.baycorpadvantage.com   Public   Access Division
Credit Reference Association of Australia
PO Box 966, NORTH SYDNEY NSW 2060

☐   Dun and Bradstreet (Australia) Pty Ltd: 13 23 33
www.dnb.com.au   Attention: Public   Access Centre
PO Box 7405, St Kilda Rd VIC 3004

The Australian Crime Commission
The Australian Crime Commission operates an Identity Fraud intelligence facility that can assist victims in notifying some Australian and State government agencies that their identity has been stolen.

Tel: (02) 6243-6666

Sample blocking letter for credit agencies
Date
Your Name
Your Address
Your City, State, Zip Code

Complaint Department
Name of Consumer Reporting Company
Address
City, State, Zip Code
Dear Sir or Madam:
I am a victim of identity theft. I am writing to request that you block the following fraudulent information in my file. This information does not relate to any transaction that I have made. The items also are circled on the attached copy of the report I received. (Identify item(s) to be blocked by name of source, such as creditors or tax court, and identify type of item, such as credit account, judgment, etc.)
Enclosed is a copy of the law enforcement report regarding my identity theft?
Please let me know if you need any other information from me to block this information on my credit report.
Sincerely,
Your name
Enclosures: (List what you are enclosing.)

Sample dispute letter for existing accounts
Date
Your Name
Your Address
Your City, State, Zip Code
Your Account Number
Name of Creditor
Billing Inquiries
Address
City, State, Zip Code
Dear Sir or Madam:

I am writing to dispute a fraudulent (charge or debit) on my account in the amount of $_____. I am a victim of identity theft, and I did not make this (charge or debit). I am requesting that the (charge be removed or the debit reinstated), that any finance and other charges related to the fraudulent amount be credited, as well, and that I receive an accurate statement.

Enclosed are copies of (use this sentence to describe any enclosed information, such as a police report) supporting my position. Please investigate this matter and correct the fraudulent (charge or debit) as soon as possible.

Sincerely,

Your name

Enclosures: (List what you are enclosing.)

Identity theft affidavit

Name _____

Phone number _____

ID Theft Affidavit

Victim Information

My full legal name is

_____

_____

(First) (Middle) (Last) (Jr., Sr., III)

(If different from above) When the events described in this affidavit took place, I was known as

_____

_____

(First) (Middle) (Last) (Jr., Sr., III)

(3) My date of birth is _____

(day/month/year)

(4) My Social Security number is
_____

(5) My driver's license or identification card state and number are
_____

(6) My current address is
_____

City _____ State _____
Zip Code _____
(7) I have lived at this address since
_____ (month/year)
(8) (If different from above) When the events described in this affidavit took place, my address was

_____

City   _____   State

_____
Zip Code _____
(9) I lived at the address in Item 8 from
_____ until (month/year)
_____ (month/year)
(10) My daytime telephone number is
(____)_____
My evening telephone number is

(____)_____
How the Fraud Occurred
Circle all that apply for items 11 - 17:
(11) I did not authorize anyone to use my name or personal information to seek the money, credit, loans, goods or services described in this report.
(12) I did not receive any benefit, money, goods or services as a result of the events described in this report.

(13) My identification documents (for example, credit cards; birth certificate; driver's license; Social Security card; etc.) were _ stolen _ lost on or about
_____. (Day/month/year)
(14) To the best of my knowledge and belief, the following person(s) used my information (for example, my name, address, date of birth, existing account numbers, Social Security number, mother's maiden name, etc.) or identification documents to get money, credit, loans, goods or services without my knowledge or authorization:

_____

Name (if known)

_____

Address (if known)

_____

Phone number(s) (if known)

_____

_____

Additional information (if known)

_____

Name (if known)

_____

Address (if known)

_____

Phone number(s) (if known)

_____

_____

Additional information (if known)
(15) I do NOT know who used my information or identification documents to get money, credit,

loans, goods or services without my knowledge or authorization.

(16) Additional comments: (For example, descriptions of the fraud, which documents or information were used or how the identity thief gained access to your information.)

_____

_____

_____

_____

(Attach additional pages as necessary.)

Victim's Law Enforcement Actions

Circle One

(17) (I am) (am not) willing to assist in the prosecution of the person(s) who committed this fraud.

Circle One

(18) (I am) (am not) authorizing the release of this information to law enforcement for the purpose of assisting them in the investigation and prosecution of the person(s) who committed this fraud.

Circle One

(19) (I have) (have not) reported the events described in this affidavit to the police or other law enforcement agency.

The police (did) (did not) write a report. In the event you have contacted the police or other law enforcement agency, please complete the following:

_____

(Agency #1)

_____

(Officer/Agency personnel taking report)

_____
(Date of report)

_____
(Report number, if any)

_____

_____
(Phone number)

_____
(Email address, if any)

_____
(Agency #2)

_____
(Officer/Agency personnel taking report)

_____
(Date of report)

_____
(Report number, if any)

_____
(Phone number)

_____
(Email address, if any)

Documentation Checklist

Please indicate the supporting documentation you are able to provide to the companies you plan to notify. Attach copies (NOT originals) to the affidavit before sending it to the companies.

(20) A copy of a valid government-issued photo-identification card (for example, your driver's license, state-issued ID card or your passport). If you are under 16 and don't have a photo-ID, you may submit a copy of your birth certificate or a copy of your official school records showing your enrollment and place of residence.

(21) Proof of residency during the time the disputed bill occurred, the loan was made or the other event took place (for example, a rental/lease agreement in your name, a copy of a utility bill or a copy of an insurance bill).

(22) A copy of the report you filed with the police or sheriff's department. If you are unable to obtain a report or report number from the police, please indicate that in Item 19. Some companies only need the report number, not a copy of the report. You may want to check with each company.

Signature

I certify that, to the best of my knowledge and belief, all the information on and attached to this affidavit is true, correct, and complete and made in good faith.

I also understand that is affidavit or the information it contains may be made available to federal, state, and/or local law enforcement agencies for such action within their jurisdiction as they deem appropriate.

I understand that knowingly making any false or fraudulent statement or representation to the government may constitute a violation of 18 U.S.C. §1001 or other federal, state, or local criminal statutes, and may result in imposition of a fine or imprisonment or both.

_____

(Signature)

_____

(Date signed)

_____

(Notary)

[Check with each company. Creditors sometimes require notarization. If they do not, please have one witness (non-relative) sign below that you completed and signed this affidavit.]
Witness:

_____

(Signature)

_____

(Printed name)

_____

(Date)

_____

(Telephone number)

It's a daunting process to be sure and one that will take quite some time to resolve, but it can be resolved. You can reclaim your identity! How do you prevent it from happening again?

Contact your local police for instruction if the information for your country is not listed or is incorrect.

Chapter Six
Accessing your credit information

Who has the right to access your credit information?

It can be difficult to determine WHO has the right to access your information. This is especially true in situations where you are requested to divulge information such as Social Security Numbers (for employment or rentals). Who has the right to demand that information and do you have the right to refuse?

You may also be concerned with who is accessing your information within businesses or government agencies. Understanding the need for your information can help you judge whether providing it is in your best interest.

While information such as your name, date of birth, mother's maiden name, address etc. are easily traced it is your SSN that is the biggest threat. If thieves know your SSN they can access your banking information, utilities and other personal information as well as establish new credit in your name.

Although originally the SSN was only to be used for Social Security programs it is now commonly used for filing purposes including bank accounts, employee, student and medical records. This makes your SSN a free pass gaining access to your personal information.

Who should require your SSN?

There are some government agencies (tax, welfare, Medicare and motor vehicles) who can lawfully require your SSN. Other agencies may request your SSN in a manner that implies you must give it.

You can determine whether the agency has a right to your SSN by reading the disclosure statement that is mandatory on government forms requesting the number. The disclosure statement will tell you if the SSN is required or optional. It also states which agency is requiring the number and what it will be used for. Government agencies have strict laws about the use and storage of SSNs – private agencies or businesses do not.

You cannot be denied services from government agencies if you refuse to give your SSN unless they are legally required to obtain it or had a law in effect before January 1, 1975 requiring SSN.

Employers must obtain your SSN to report earnings and payroll taxes. While they are required by law to have your SSN you might ask for them to protect your number if it is used for filing, listed on ID badges or otherwise made public.

Other businesses or agencies, including private medical insurance and schools, may request your SSN. If they are federally funded schools or are reporting to the IRS they may have a legal right to the information. If the reason for the request is not listed on the form you can leave the space provided for your SSN blank and ask for an explanation of why they are requesting it.

While a business may have no legal right to the information they can refuse service if you choose not to disclose it. State laws differ but businesses should not willfully display SSNs, however, carelessness or inadequate protection of SSNs may not violate these laws.

Financial information that is of interest to the IRS requires your SSN to be listed. Banking, stocks, employment and other financial statements all must include the number.

Credit card companies may request your SSN but are not legally required to have it. Since the number is used to validate who you are you may be able to provide proof with other forms of identification. Be prepared to have a difficult time finding a creditor who will provide credit if you refuse to submit your SSN.

Since potential creditors (including landlords) may wish to see your credit report you will likely be required to give them your SSN to obtain the report. You may ask if they will accept a current report without the SSN and confirm your identity with other forms of ID.

Federal records, including driver's license, divorce papers, child support and death certificates all require SSNs. Birth certificates usually require the SSNs of both of the parents unless there is good cause for not requiring it.

If you receive email that appears to be from a service provider or government agency that requests your SSN do not reply. This information will not be requested through unsolicited emails and is being sent from a fraudulent source.

You can find out more about the legal requirements for using your SSN at:

http://www.privacy.ca.gov/recommendations/snrecommendations.pdf

What have you done to protect your privacy?
In the US activities of the FTC to combat identity theft include but not limited to the following:

In February 2013, FTC released several videos to help compute users protect their personal information online. Tips on how to stay safe while using public Wi-Fi hotspots, shopping online, using public computers were shared. These instruction videos could be found on OnGuardOnline.gov. FTC further reminds consumers to be wary of identity thieves while filing in their tax return which normally contains sensitive and personal information. FTC also recommended steps to take if anyone thinks he has been a victim of identity theft.

In July 2013 FTC held free identity theft webinar for the blind and visually impaired on how to protect themselves from identity theft. It was tagged "Talking through identity theft", a program for the Blind and Visually Impaired". It covered the financial medical and government sectors as well as issues facing children and older adults in dealing with identity theft.

In January 2014, FTC hosted 16 different events across the country along with a series of national webinar and twitter chats designed to raise awareness about tax identity theft. They also provided consumers with tips on how to protect themselves and what to do if they become victims.

In October 2014 the chairperson of the FTC issued a statement reinforcing the government's initiative to safeguard consumers' financial security. According to her, "Identity theft has been American consumers' number one complaint for more than a decade, and it affects people in every community across the nation. I welcome the opportunity for the Federal Trade Commission to participate in this new initiative advancing efforts to address this insidious problem on behalf of consumers."

In December 2014 FTC released a video advice to computer users to back up their data files at least once a week. This was to be a New Year resolution for the year 2015.

In January 2015 FTC began the year's war against identity theft by hosting identity theft awareness for a whole week to raise awareness about the scam that puts thousands of consumers at risk every year.

In May 2015 the FTC launched a new resource for identity theft victims. The website IdentityTheft.gov makes it easier for identity theft victims to report and recover from identity theft. A Spanish version of the site is also available at Robodeldentidad.gov.

In January 2016 FTC further equipped IdentityTheft.gov with an array of new tools for identity theft victims for recovery plans and assistance to alert the police.

Oct 2016 the FTC hosted an all-day conference, "Planning for the Future," examining the state of identity theft now and how it may evolve in the future, in Washington, DC.

July 20117, FTC held 2017 Military Consumer Financial Workshop: "Protecting Those Who Protect Our Nation". It examined financial issues and scams that affect military consumers, including active duty service members in all branches and veterans. The workshop also discussed FTC resources available to military consumer advocates and representatives on financial readiness and fraud prevention, including the FTC's Military Consumer Toolkit, available at Military.Consumer.gov. The toolkit allows personal financial managers, counselors, and others in the military community to share practical financial readiness tips and can be individually customized and easily shared on social media.

2017 will marked the ten-year anniversary of the executive order creating the federal Identity

Theft Task Force, which was co-chaired by the FTC. Despite numerous advances in combating identity theft, it remains a top consumer complaint each year to the FTC, and Department of Justice statistics show that millions of consumers are victims of identity theft.

Cifas is the fraud prevention body in the UK. Services provided include identity protection, internal fraud database, national fraud database and payment account database. Cifas now publishes Fraudscape where fraud statistics including identity theft are revealed ever year.

According to Cifas, identity theft figures show that identity fraud was highest in 2016 with 173,000 cases reported. Identity theft thus continued to be the number one fraud threat in the UK.

Figures released by Cifas include 2016 – 172,919 cases of identity theft, 2015 – 169,592, 2014 – 113,839, 2013 – 108,554, 2012 – 123,589, 2011 – 113,589 and 2010 – 102,672.

Cifas also gave tips on how to prevent identity theft as well as what to do if you are a victim. Among their recommendation was to contact: crimestoppers 0800555111, www.crimestoppers-uk.org; victim support at www.victimsupport.org.uk and also report to Action Fraud 03001232040, www.actionfraud.police.uk/

Cifas encourages people to register with the organization for safer internet experience especially it offers protective registration for individuals whose identities are at risk of being used fraudulently, for instance after a burglary. In 2014 Cifas launched a scheme called

Protection the Vulnerable free of charge to certain groups of vulnerable people whose identity may have been at risk.

Cifas work with other organizations like HMG's Cyber streetwise Campaign, City of London and action Fraud, Get Safe Online, Financial Fraud action UK to enlighten individuals about identity fraud in order to reduce the menace.

Despite all these efforts, identity theft has been on the rise for a consecutive 13 years in the US. According to a survey by the FTC, in 2010 it accounted for 15% of complaints lodged with FTC in 2011 it rose to 24% and in 2012 43%. Every year since 1997, the Consumer Sentinel Network (CSN) publishes fraud and identity theft complaints which has risen more than 13 million complaints at the end 2016.

The big question is what are you doing to protect your identity?

While government agencies are submitted to legal requirements that protect your personal information, other businesses are not. This makes it vitally important to take steps protecting your information yourself and knowing who has it and what they are doing with it.

State laws do have requirements for the disposal of personal records but the manner of disposal can vary depending on the nature of the information and the resources available to the business. If you do business which requires you to keep personal information on record you must check with local law regarding the disposal of these records.

While the law is still catching up to the needs of individual privacy protection, Europe, Canada and the USA have created a guideline of processes for collecting and using personal information. This guide is called the 'Fair Information Practice Principles'. It outlines the safeguards necessary to ensure the use of personal information is fair and to protect privacy.

The core principles outlined in the Fair Information Practice Principles are: Notice/Awareness; Choice/Consent; Access/Participation; Integrity/Security; and Enforcement/Redress.

Here is a brief outline of these principles:

Notice/Awareness

Notice and awareness requires businesses requesting personal information to disclose their information practices before collecting information. The following principles listed would be included in the notice.

Choice/Consent

Choice and consent give the individual the ability to allow or restrict the use of personal information beyond the transaction being initiated. Opt-in or opt-out choices include how much personal information is included and what it may be used for.

Access/Participation

Access and participation requires the individual to be able to access, correct or verify their personal information on record. The means of accessing and making corrections must be timely and inexpensive.

Integrity/Security

Integrity and security refer to the business' steps to maintain accurate records, secure the information and destroy records in an appropriate manner.

Enforcement/Redress

Enforcement and redress must be established either by self-regulation or legislation.

The full report of Fair Information Practice Principles can be found at:
http://www.ftc.gov/reports/privacy3/fairinfo.htm.

While steps are being made to create enforcement it is up to the individual to be aware of the use and protection provided by each business and agency they provide personal information to.

Chapter Seven
Prevent identity fraud

What can you do to prevent identity theft?

When it comes to identity theft, you can't entirely control whether you will become a victim. But there are certain steps you can take to minimize recurrences.

Are you familiar with the expression "an ounce of prevention is worth a pound of cure"? This is absolutely true in regards to protecting your identity from being stolen rather than dealing with the trauma and cost of being a victim.

It must be re-stated here that there are no guarantees that the steps you take will prevent your identity from being stolen. Personal information is available from sources (including government, employment and other business records) that we are not in a position to personally protect.

Taking steps to limit the use of our personal information makes it more difficult to become a target. Proper disposal of personal records and other common sense steps will also thwart any opportunistic thieves.

Here are some steps that every individual should incorporate into the management of their personal information. What you choose to implement will depend on how much time or energy you want to use in protecting your information. Making conscious decisions as to how or when our personal information is shared will give us more control and should become a lifelong habit.

Monitor your credit reports

The first and possibly most important thing consumers can do to protect their identity is to monitor their credit reports. A recent amendment to the federal Fair Credit Reporting Act requires each of the major nationwide consumer reporting companies to provide you with a free copy of your credit reports, at your request, once every 12 months.

To request a copy of your free credit report, visit www.annualcreditreport.com or call toll-free 1-877-322-8228. Do not contact the credit reporting companies directly. They only provide free reports through the above web address and phone number.

If you notice anything wrong on your report, refer to the section on correcting your credit report to take the appropriate steps to have the information removed or amended. You will also want to investigate thoroughly your other financial accounts to be sure the problems don't extend to other areas.

In places where you are entitled to one free credit report direct from credit agencies each year you can request a report every four months by requesting one from each of the three credit agencies in turn. It is wise to check your credit report at least once every year even if you must pay to receive it. If you suspect your identity has been stolen or have received notice of information that has been stolen you may be able to get free reports throughout the first year of the incident. The risk of identity theft is too serious to be left to free expense and chance. For a token major credit reference agencies are happy to watch over your credit movement online and advice you round the year. Most credit reference agencies in the UK allows you 30 days free trial period to access your credit report and online activities before charging you for their services. This period will enable you familiarize yourself with their protection and services before committing your money.

Don't carry your SSN/NI in your wallet

Social Security Numbers, National Insurance Numbers (UK), birth certificates, passports, biometrics or any other personal identification should not be carried in your wallet. The same goes for extra credit cards and store or gas credit cards. The less you carry the less risk if your wallet is stolen or lost. Don't carry your Social

Security card with you; leave it in a secure place.

Give your SSN only when absolutely necessary, and ask to use other types of identifiers. If your state uses your SSN as your driver's license number, ask to substitute another number. Do the same if your health insurance company uses your SSN as your policy number.

Carry only the identification information and the credit and debit cards that you'll actually need when you go out. Keep your purse or wallet in a safe place at work; do the same with copies of administrative forms that have your sensitive personal information.

Stop pre-approved credit offers

You can stop the mailing of pre-approved credit offers by calling toll-free 888-5OPTOUT (888-567-8688). Ask to have your name removed from the list as pre-approved credit offers can be easily abused by thieves. You could as well call the credit card companies and demand that your details be taken off their database. You may be asked to provide your SSN which the consumer reporting companies need to match you with your file.

Shred personal documents

Treat your mail and trash carefully. Deposit your outgoing mail in post office collection boxes or at your local post office, rather than in an unsecured mailbox. Promptly remove mail from your mailbox. If you're planning to be away from home and can't pick up your mail, contact your local Post Office to request a vacation hold. They will hold your mail there until you can pick it up or are home to receive it.

To thwart an identity thief who may pick through your trash or recycling bins to capture your personal information, tear or shred your charge receipts, copies of credit applications, insurance forms, physician statements, checks and bank statements, expired charge cards that you're discarding, and credit offers you get in the mail.

If you do throw away pre-approved credit offers or other personal information (such as old tax forms, bank statements or expired credit cards) you must shred the information before disposing it. This will stop impostors from covertly contacting the credit companies and accepting the offer on your behalf.

Pick up the mail every day

Don't allow mail to sit overnight in the mail box or you give thieves an easy target. Credit card offers, bank statements and possibly information with your SSN/NI can be used to open new credit in your name or steal from you.

Don't respond to email requests

Be cautious when responding to promotions. Identity thieves may create phony promotional offers to get you to give them your personal information.

I once had a co-worker who made copies of everything in his wallet once a month and kept them in a secure place inside his home. This is a great idea to easily help you keep track of credit cards (copy the front and back), checking account numbers, and health insurance information (again front and back copies).

If you are contacted by a bank or service provider through email you must never submit any personal or financial information to them. These attempts to 'trick' you into believing they are a legitimate business are called *phishing*. This trick is like fishing where baits are thrown out with a metal hook concealed underneath. The moment the bait is swallowed, such one is hooked and the rest is left to imagination.

If an email claims that you must validate your information and provides you a link to the form DO NOT OPEN THE LINK! If you are concerned that the request may be legitimate close the email and enter the URL to the actual business in your browser window. If your account looks fine contact their customer service department to verify the email. A fraudulent email is called a 'spoof' and the company will likely want you to forward it to them.

Don't give information to phone callers

Unless you initiate a call to a business you should never give personal or financial information to a caller over the phone. Your bank or Credit Card Company will not ask for your card or account number if they call you. They have that information on file. Most banks give this advice on their website that they will never ask you for your personal information on phone or online. They encourage their customers to ignore such requests and report them to the bank. A number of banks have secure message sections on their website where you send them private and secure messages.

If a caller portrays themselves to be representing a charity or offering a prize or trip you can ask for a phone number to call back. Verify the phone number and hang up. If they are with a reputable organization you will be able to check the number and call back. Different sites like 'SayNoTo087 offer both free information and alternative phone numbers of businesses and government organizations.

Telemarketing scams that ask for credit card deposits, account information or personal information such as your mother's maiden name, your SSN or other information are common. If you wish to donate it is better to call the organization yourself.

Put passwords on your credit cards

As we said earlier, be aware when billing statements don't arrive when they should, if you receive credit cards you didn't ask for, and if you've been denied credit for no apparent reason. These are all signs of identity theft.

Place passwords on your credit card, bank, and phone accounts. Avoid using easily available information like your mother's maiden name, your birth date, the last four digits of your SSN or your phone number, or a series of consecutive numbers. When opening new accounts, you may find that many businesses still have a line on their applications for your mother's maiden name. Ask if you can use a password instead.

Credit card companies like Visa offer added protection by allowing you to create a password or memorable words along with the card number when making a purchase. Even if your card is stolen you can prevent thieves from using it by having it password protected. Each time you contact your credit card company, they ask you to verify the password or memorable word in order for them to know that you are the genuine owner of the account.

Be aware of who has access
Secure personal information in your home, especially if you have roommates, employ outside help, or are having work done in your home.

Consider using a post office box instead of home mail delivery to minimize the chances of mail theft.

Ask about information security procedures in your workplace or at businesses, doctor's offices or other institutions that collect your personally identifying information. Find out who has access to your personal information and verify that it is handled securely. Ask about the disposal procedures for those records as well. Find out if your information will be shared with anyone else. If so, ask how your information can be kept confidential.

If you are a member of the military and away from your usual duty station, you may place an active duty alert on your credit reports to help minimize the risk of identity theft while you are deployed. Active duty alerts are in effect on your report for one year. If your deployment lasts longer, you can place another alert on your credit report.

When you place an active duty alert, you'll be removed from the credit reporting companies' marketing list for pre-screened credit card offers for two years unless you ask to go back on the list before then. You can have an authorized agent do this for you, but make sure they have the proper authorization documentation to do so.

Don't give out personal information through the mail, or on the Internet unless you've initiated the contact or are sure you know who you're dealing with. Identity thieves are clever, and have posed as representatives of banks, Internet service providers (ISPs), and even government agencies to get people to reveal their SSN, mother's maiden name, account numbers, and other identifying information.

Before you share any personal information, confirm that you are dealing with a legitimate organization. Check an organization's website by typing its URL in the address line, rather than cutting and pasting it. Many companies post scam alerts when their name is used improperly. Or call customer service using the number listed on your account statement or in the telephone book.

Don't give passwords to credit cards or other personal information to friends and family. According to a survey done by www.idtheftcener.org the victim respondents indicated that 43% of them thought they knew the imposter. About 34% were aware that the thief had a history of needing money to support a drug, drinking, gambling or shopping addiction. Don't be a victim, it is better to learn from other people's experience.

When you use the ATM, be mindful of anyone around you. Cover the keypad when entering in your PIN to defeat prying eyes or miniature cameras.

Do not allow yourself to be distracted when using the ATM. That is prime time for criminals to strike.

You can physically protect yourself and your documents, but there are other ways for thieves to secure your personal operation – through your personal computer.

Chapter Eight
Safety first

In the Internet age, hackers are becoming more in number and savvier in manipulating the Internet to obtain information from users. This might make you very scared to do any business online at all, but there are measures you can take to make your surfing safe.

Virus protection software should be updated regularly, and patches for your operating system and other software programs should be installed to protect against intrusions and infections that can lead to the compromise of your computer files or passwords.

Ideally, virus protection software should be set to automatically update each week. The Windows operating system also can be set to automatically check for patches and download them to your computer.

Do not open files sent to you by strangers, or click on hyperlinks or download programs from people you don't know. Be careful about using file sharing programs. Opening a file could expose your system to a computer virus or a program known as "spyware," which could capture your passwords or any other information as you type it into your keyboard.

Be very careful, as some e-mails from companies like Pay Pal are very real looking and could bait you into opening them by thinking they are legit. A good rule of thumb with e-mails like these is to never, ever click on a link in the e-mail. If you do, you'll be prompted to enter in your information and then the thief will have it.

You should forward any suspicious e-mails like these to the company's spoof department. Usually, the address is spoof@ (company name).com). For example, spoof@paypal.com. They will usually respond back to you if the e-mail was legitimate or if it was a phisher that sent it.

Use a firewall program, especially if you use a high-speed Internet connection like cable, DSL or T-1 that leaves your computer connected to the Internet 24 hours a day. The firewall program will allow you to stop uninvited access to your computer. Without it, hackers can take over your computer, access the personal information stored on it, or use it to commit other crimes.

Use a secure browser - software that encrypts or scrambles information you send over the Internet -to guard your online transactions. Be sure your browser has the most up-to-date encryption capabilities by using the latest version available from the manufacturer.

You also can download some browsers for free over the Internet. When submitting information, look for the "lock" icon on the browser's status bar to be sure your information is secure during transmission. This will appear when you are submitting information over a secure site which will protect your information.

Also look in the web browser's address bar. Most web addresses start with

"http://". If it is a secure site, the address will be "https://"

Try not to store financial information on your laptop unless absolutely necessary. If you do, use a strong password a combination of letters (upper and lower case), numbers and symbols.

A good way to create a strong password is to think of a memorable phrase and use the first letter of each word as your password, converting some letters into numbers that resemble letters. For example, "I love Felix; he's a good cat," would become 1LFHA6c.

Don't use an automatic log-in feature that saves your user name and password, and always log off when you're finished. That way, if your laptop is stolen, it's harder for a thief to access your personal information.

Before you dispose of a computer, delete all the personal information it stored. Deleting files using the keyboard or mouse commands or reformatting your hard drive may not be enough because the files may stay on the computer's hard drive, where they may be retrieved easily. Use a "wipe" utility program to overwrite the entire hard drive.

Online shopping is easy, convenient and in fact magical. You get across the globe in a minute access all you need delivered to your door step. Nevertheless, there are inherent dangers and risk of loss in online shopping. This does not mean one has to stop shopping online; it only enjoins one to be prudent while shopping online. Only shop at merchants you are familiar with or contact the Better Business Bureau. Look for secure shopping sites with identifying marks such as https appearing in the browser window or a lock icon appearing below the webpage on your browser.

Never give PIN numbers or passwords to the merchant. Verify your bank statements immediately online or over the phone to check the transaction was made for the proper amount and no other charges were made. Be sure to have anti-virus and anti-spyware programs running and always print out the transaction record, log out and close the browser when completed.

Read more about Online Privacy in the following chapter.

Another way to protect yourself while shopping online is the use of prepaid cards. These cards enable you to limit the amount you want to spend by pre-loading the card with only the money needed. No transaction will be honoured without the amount being preloaded in the card. Therefore no imposter will be able to use your card illegally.

Always ask or opt-out

Whenever you are asked for personal information you have a right to know why it is needed and how it will be used. Online you may find that information in a Privacy Policy (read about that in the chapter 'How to Read a Privacy Policy').

Limit the use of your personal information by requesting financial institutions not to share your information with affiliates. This is called 'opting-out' and the financial institution must allow you to do so. Once you have requested to opt-out, either on the phone or in writing, they must never share your information unless you specifically request they do so.

Sign your cards immediately

When you do receive a new credit or debit card sign it immediately and never carry it unsigned. Most shopping malls may ask you to confirm your ownership of the card you used by asking you to sign your signature and then comparing it with the one at the reverse side of your card. If there is no signature at the back of your card or if the signature is irregular, this may generate disputes with the vendors. It is also easy for thieves to claim ownership of unsigned cards by inscribing their signature first.

Don't save passwords to personal information (such as online banking) in a program that 'remembers' your information. Remove cookies from your computer and have your hard drive professionally 'wiped' before disposing it. Remember that your personal computer today is going to be someone else's or recycled tomorrow. So think deeply about when the computer will pass to someone else. Several browsers like google chrome usually asks whether you want it to remember your password on the computer. While this seems to be an innocuous good gesture, the risk as it were lurks in the future when you might not be able to retract and delete such passwords.

Use strong passwords – that means a combination of letters and numbers that can't be easily guessed. Never use information such as your mother's maiden name or birth date that can be figured out by thieves.

Read more on password in the 'How to create a strong password' tips chapter.

Set your browser security settings to Medium or higher. Install a firewall to prevent unwanted access from hackers and install anti-virus and anti-spyware programs. Never download software when you don't know where it's from and never click on pop-ups or spam email. If possible, install ad blockers, empty spam folders and clean all cookies and temporary files on daily basis.

Along with the convenience of the internet has come a new wave of predators looking to steal from innocent victims. This often occurs through 'spoof' emails.

A 'spoof' email is an email that appears to be from a legitimate organization or business – often banks or service providers – but is really a fake email sent from a con artist.

These thieves construct emails that use the logos and styles of the bank or business and attempt to convince the recipient to reply or click on a link to a website and submit personal and financial information that can be used to commit identity fraud.

While these emails are extremely common they can be difficult to identify unless you know what to look for. Here are some signals that an email may be a fraud as well as some general warnings about dealing with 'spoof' emails.

Not using your name
Spoof emails will likely not have your name in the message. They may be addressed 'Dear Customer', 'Member', 'Friend' or other ambiguous title. Real emails from institutions or business you have accounts with will use your

name or a name you created for your account. Even when a purported message addresses you by name, have a close look at the address and see if there is anything strange, for example, if an email showing the logo of a bank or any organization has another email address with say Yahoo, Gmail or Hotmail instead of the bank or the organization, treat with suspicion. In addition to this any email from an institution that wants you to reply to another email address totally different from the institution should be treated with suspicion.

No account number
Companies that you have done business with will have account numbers and passwords on file. If you are ever contacted by a business that asks you to verify your account number or password, do not respond. Only give information to businesses if you have initiated the contact.

Improper Grammar or Spelling Errors
A surprising amount of these 'spoofs' will have grammar or spelling errors. Whether this is because the con artist is not a native English speaker or it was done in a hurry is immaterial. A legitimate business email will not likely have these glaring errors.

Warnings to close your account
Often the 'spoof' email takes the form of a warning that your account has been illegally accessed, that you have been a victim of fraud or that your account will be closed unless you respond to the email. They will ask you to click

on a link in the email and verify your information. In reality you are giving the information to the thief who will use it to access your real accounts.

Always be suspicious of emails that ask for personal information. Contact the business through their official website and find out how to forward the fraudulent email to them. If you have opened any links or provided personal information you should immediately contact the business about the account and watch for unauthorized activity. Change all passwords or close the accounts and open new ones with different access codes.

'Phishing' emails
'Spoofs' are also called 'phishing' emails. 'Phishing' refers to any email that attempts to get you to share personal or financial information that can be used to commit fraud.

While 'spoofs' pretend to be a known business or institution, 'phishing' emails also include offers to collect prizes, requests for help, charity donations or false notices that you have won a lottery or a trip. They tell you that to reserve your prize you must give them a credit card number for verification or as a deposit.
Some emails request your help by offering you a portion of a fund that will be deposited into your bank account. These are often sent as requests from rich foreign nobility or government officials. They are dangerous groups and should never be contacted or replied to.

Similar scams are also done over the telephone and are called 'pretexting'. Always contact the organization or business directly if you are contacted for charitable donations or account information.

Chapter Nine
Online privacy

Special concern: Online privacy

While many suggestions have already been listed to protect your identity online there are a few areas that require special attention.

Email Fraud
Email fraud was thoroughly explained in the preceding chapter about steps to take to prevent identity fraud. Treat every unsolicited email with suspicion and exercise caution when sending information that contains personal or financial details through email. It is advisable to further increase the level of suspicion when the email has any kind of attachment. Attachments that are not scanned from the source may actually be trailed by viruses or spyware.

Protect your computer
Computer viruses and spyware can enter your computer when you click on a link in an email

or by accessing a website that downloads the program without your consent.

While no person can prevent all exposure to these viruses and spyware you can protect your computer by installing a firewall as well as purchasing anti-virus and anti-spyware programs that routinely search your computer and remove these threats.

Viruses can spread through your computer, corrupting files and information as well as being passed on to other people through your email. Spyware can track your movements on the internet as well as collect information that you enter while using the internet including passwords, banking information and personal data.

You may also download programs that appear safe but are hiding spyware or viruses. These programs are called Trojan Horses. Only download information from sites you know and trust.

Shop securely

Online shopping is convenient but can also pose hazards for unwary buyers. While electronic exchange of funds makes buying online easier it is important to watch for signs of a secure site. Secure sites provide encryption of data so that others can't view it or intercept it. This encryption is called SSL (Secure Socket Layers).

Look for security symbols such as a closed padlock on the bottom of your browser window and URLs that start with *https* instead of http. Http stands for hypertext transfer protocol while https means hyper text transfer protocol secure.

The difference is the additional security provided by the https. It is the communication protocol for secure transmission over a computer network which is widely used on the internet. Encryption that hides your sensitive information (like passwords, credit card numbers and other personal data) by displaying it as dots rather than the actual numbers or letters is another safety feature.

Check the Privacy Policy and only deal with reputable merchants. Check with the Better Business Bureau if you're unsure. You may also consider third party payment processors (such as PayPal and ClickBank) which prevent the merchant from obtaining any financial information directly. Check the security status and privacy policies of any third party processor before making a transaction.

Sharing computers or using laptops

If you are sending personal information on a public or shared computer you must log out of the browser before ending your session. If you don't log out another person may be able to use the back button on the browser to obtain your information. Empty cookies so other users will not be given your information if they access the same site. Check the downloads, temporary files as well and empty the recycle bin. If possible in addition to login out, shut down and restart the computer before leaving.

Storing personal information on personal computers (especially laptops) can be dangerous if the computer is stolen or hacked (illegally accessed). Don't save sensitive passwords in programs that can auto-fill forms. Although auto-fill is a great help in making your job faster when completing an online form, it is advisable to skip out a number of details like passwords and pins when using auto-fills.

Online forums and chat rooms

You may find that in the excitement of meeting new people and developing personal relationships in online forums and chat rooms you often forget the dangers of providing too much information.

In these social or business gatherings you may foster friendships within the group but it is important to remember that these areas are available to the public and individuals who are not making their presence known can still be 'lurking' on the forums and searching for personal pieces of information that are inadvertently expressed.

You never really know who you are talking to so it is wise to make it a habit to never reveal personal information such as your telephone number or address to these public groups.

Even if you are dealing with a private chat room you should exercise caution if you are not personally familiar with the individual(s) you are speaking too. Misrepresentation happens often enough to make it a real danger even for adults. Never send personal or financial information to individuals in a chat room or on a forum.

The anonymity of the internet can cause people to say things online that they would never say in person. It is wise to avoid getting involved in heated debates (also called "flame wars" or "flaming" when directed to a particular individual). People online are just as real as those you meet in the flesh and saying something to incite another person can be just as dangerous online as offline.

Watch where you're going

Don't download anything when you don't trust the source. Even if you are emailed or given a link in a chat room or forum you should be cautious. Look at the URL. Some links will directly download programs – including viruses – without your consent.

While using anti-virus and anti-spyware programs will help avoid problems they can't catch everything. Know where you're going and who is sending you. Even when you think you know who is sending stuff to you, enough care should still be exercised as the person sending you the link might as well got it from a friend without sufficient checks and assurance. Care and suspicion are the watchwords.

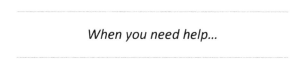

When you need help...

If you need help dealing with online security issues including harassment or fraud you can contact the Cyber Law Enforcement Organization at: http://www.cyberlawenforcement.org/ or check out more information at http://www.wiredsafety.org/ or http://www.id theftcenter.org/ vresources.shtml.

While these organizations have connections to legal or volunteer assistance you should contact your local police if you suspect your identity has been stolen or fear for your safety.

Chapter Ten
Safer with strong
passwords

How to create a strong password

It's almost funny if it weren't so sad that many people still use their birthdays and sometimes names of favorite family members as their passwords. A good password is one that is *impossible* to guess. Many people know this already, but only a few truly understand the importance of creating a strong, impossible-to-guess password.

So why do you need a strong password?
Your password is what you need in order to prove to the computer that you are who you say you are. It functions like a normal house key, except that instead of carrying it around in your pocket or your wallet, you carry it around in your head.

Like a regular house key, passwords can be stolen. Someone using your password will pretend to be you in order to gain access to your account, files, or any other important information you store in your computer or database.

The computer has no way of knowing if it is really you or someone pretending to be you, the same way that your door has no way of knowing if it is you holding that key inserted into the keyhole.

For these reasons, it is important to safeguard a password, and one of the most reliable ways of safeguarding your password is to create one that is difficult to crack. So you will create highly complicated passwords – unfathomable letter combinations and numbers and symbols and upper case letters and lower case letters and whatever else you can add into the whole mix.

However, the main trouble about password security is that people will have to remember them in order to gain access to the network, whether it is a home computer network or an office network.

Now, if you were using a literal cocktail of letters, symbols, and numbers as a password, you would have to have exceptionally high capacity for remembering codes. The problem is not all people have brains that function like that.

In fact, most people are better at remembering words that actually make sense than a splatter of alphanumeric with who-knows-what meaning. As such, people naturally prefer the former when choosing or creating passwords.

Unfortunately, hackers are very, very smart. If, given enough computing power, time, and encrypted data, these hackers can compromise even the most complex cryptographic system, how much more a password that is easy to crack? It is like stealing candy from a baby, to borrow a line.

The purpose therefore of creating strong passwords is to make it as difficult as possible for the hacker to figure out, even if he had all the time in the world to crack it.

However, taking into account our admittedly human tendency to remember things in context, your password should also be one that you can relatively recall fairly easily – that is, they should not be completely alien to the brain, like all numeric codes, to make them easier to remember and store in our memory banks.

In fact, experts in network security highly encourage that you use a combination of numeric codes and letters of the alphabet as this will increase the number of odds and make it more difficult for the hacker to figure out the right combination.

Passwords to avoid

Okay, you have to admit that there are only so many words that people use and so many numbers that it is difficult to come up with something totally original to make use of as a password.

More often than not, people will use the same password for all their accounts without even knowing that some other person in some other state or country is also using the same password because they thought it was unique.

Moreover, hackers use cracking devices specifically for the purpose of figuring out people's passwords. These devices will run a list of all possible letter and number combinations and then all the hacker has to do is to try out each one until he gets the right one.

It seems like a tedious job, but cracking devices are actually very sophisticated software that can eliminate all the other odds in order to get the hacker closer to figuring out the right password. They have resources and a deep understanding of how people think (at least, when it comes to what passwords the average Joe would likely pick up) to make the whole task simple.

Now, couple that with all the wonderful technology at their disposal, and you are practically at their mercy, unless you take steps in avoiding the following weak passwords:

Words in the dictionary, including any dictionary in any language or technical application (e.g. engineering dictionary)

Your username or your real name
Your spouse's name or the name of any person you know, including family members
(This is because password crackers can easily get a list of 10,000 names or more and then run them through your system to see if one works)

Words found in the "cracking dictionary"
(Yes, password crackers do keep a list of words that a lot of people use. This includes abbreviations; cartoons; character patterns;

asteroids; famous names; Bible; movies; god, myths and legends; Password (the word itself); female names; male names; machine names; science fiction; songs; sports; number patterns; surnames; places; short phrases; Shakespeare; etc.

Any common words with a single character before or after it (e.g. 1happy, Paris8)

Any common words, capitalized (e.g., Soccer)

Any common words, reversed (e.g., soccer → reccos), doubled (e.g., soccer → soccersoccer), or mirrored (e.g., soccer → soccerreccos)

There was a time when it was a good idea to take a word and substitute some of the characters.

For instance, instead of using the word "password," you can make it into this alphanumeric combination: P@$$w0rd. This is actually a good password, as far as the rules of creating good passwords are concerned. However, there are actually some cracking devices today that are designed to crack even those kinds of passwords, so you probably should not take this route anymore.

Now that you know what passwords to avoid, time for you to learn what makes a good password.

Rules for creating a strong password

One of the first things to remember when creating strong passwords is the balance between coming up with a password that is complex enough to give crackers a hard time, yet easy enough for the user to recall. This should be too difficult if you take note of the following tips:

The six-character rule
A strong password should be one that is composed of six characters or more. This will make it difficult for a hacker to crack with a brute-force attack.

You can use as many characters as you like so long as you meet the minimum of six characters. However, note that there are some systems that establish a maximum number of characters. For instance, the UNIX system has a maximum of eight characters.

Upper and lower case combination
This was mentioned earlier. Passwords are made case-sensitive for a reason, and that is reason is to increase the security level of gaining access to your account. But in addition to upper and lower case combinations, strong passwords should also incorporate punctuation marks and numbers.

Now, one common mistake people make when it comes to passwords like this is they write it down to help them remember. While these passwords are admittedly hard to recall, DO NOT make the mistake of writing them down anywhere or keeping a record of them anywhere in your system.

The license plate rule

This rule is simple. Just take a word or a phrase and then squeeze it into six or eight characters the way you would with a vanity license plate.

Small words and punctuation marks
The good thing about passwords like these is that they are easy to come up with and easy to remember. Let's take the word "coffee" for instance. Take that word and insert punctuation marks in there somewhere to mess up the crackers – i.e. "co%ff*ee"

Use control characters
This can be a good choice. However, note that there are some that bear special meanings. For instance, characters like ^U, ^H, or ^D might prevent you from logging in again.

Use uncommon phrase
Remember this rule: short phrases are a no-no. But uncommon phrases tweaked just so are okay. More than okay, in fact.

For example, let's take a Latin legal phrase: "Dura lex sed lex", which means "the law may be hard but it is the law." Now, take the last letters of each word to get this combination: "axdx." Finally, throw in a capital letter, punctuation marks, and numbers and you can come up with a hard-to-crack password like this: "Ax%d3x*"

Misspelling rule

Deliberately misspelling words is highly encouraged. This will make your password harder to crack.

Random gambit
And last but not least, try to come up with a password that is totally random to anyone else but not to you.

We can't tell you how to come up with these because then if we ourselves can figure it out, then it's probably not that random. So only you can really come up with random passwords that are difficult to crack. Just think hard and...USE YOUR IMAGINATION.

And once you have come up with a good, strong password using the above-given tips, the next important step is to continuously update your password. Six months is the maximum length of time you should keep using a password. Experts agree that this is the optimum period with which a password will remain secure and uncompromised. It will also take this long for a typical cracking device to crack your strong password.

Chapter Eleven
Public privacy policies

Learn how to read a privacy policy

One of the essential steps to protecting your privacy is understanding how to read a privacy policy.

Privacy policies should be made available in some form anytime you are asked to provide personal information. Financial institutions, health facilities or other businesses that collect your information can be asked to show you their privacy policy before you give them your information.

If the company does not have privacy policies, consider doing business elsewhere. It is a show of respect to customers to tell them how their information will be used.

Online you will find privacy policies posted on websites. The privacy policy is an indication of the steps they will take to protect your identity or to inform you of how they will treat the information you provide. Simply having a privacy policy does not guarantee you any level of protection. To understand what is protected and what is shared you must read the policy.

Each site has its own criteria for a privacy policy. Some give full protection including encryption of passwords and not providing your information to any third party while others tell you that your information will be shared with affiliated companies or businesses they feel you would be interested in hearing from. You must read the policy to be aware of the steps being taken to protect you. So each time you got to the point of agreeing to a policy or form, watch out for the terms and condition as well as the privacy policy and right-click to display in a new window. You can as well copy it out and increase the font to enable you read it properly. If in doubt, print out the privacy policy statement and put the agreement or form on hold until you are able to clarify your doubt.

Here are some of the items to look for on a privacy policy:

What information is collected and why?
When a business is requesting personal information it is reasonable to ask what information is collected and why it is needed. If they request information that doesn't seem relevant they should state why they need it.

If there is no explanation for the request try to avoid giving the additional information or ask them why they need it. Asking for your income or the name of your spouse is the kind of information you might question providing without reasonable cause.

How is the information collected?

While filling out paper forms is straight forward you need to find out from websites how the information is being collected. Websites sometimes use cookies that they install on the visitor's computer to track information about what pages they click on, how long they spend there and your IP address.

This information can be tracked without your consent. Usually it is only to facilitate the company's marketing research or to assist you by using your information from previous visits. You should be able to find out what information is automatically stored by reading the privacy policy. Several websites display the warning: "we use cookies" and ask you to learn more in order to get more information about their cookie policy before you consent.

Please see the chapter on cookies to learn more.

What will the information be used for?

If the business asks for your personal or financial information you have a right to know what it will be used for. Is it only to complete the transaction? Will they view a purchase as permission to market to you again or to sell your information to other businesses? Also how long they are going to store your information may be part of the policy. This information should be available in the privacy policy as well as information on how to 'opt-out' of these uses.

Who will have access to your information?

Is the information sold or rented? Do they share your name, email address or purchasing habits with other businesses? These areas should be clearly outlined in the privacy policy. If they do sell or rent the names on their list you may wish to limit the information you provide. Although no institution will own up to that fact that they do sell or rent out your information, there are certain watchwords to look out for.

Watch for terms like "affiliates", "sponsors" or "partners" since you will have no idea who will be receiving the information.

How secure is your information?

What steps are taken to protect your personal information? Any transaction that requires you to submit personal or financial information should have SSL (Secure Socket Layers). SSL will encrypt the information so that it can't be read by others during transmission.

You can verify the security by looking for the *https* at the beginning of the URL and an icon with a lock (closed) in the bottom corner of your browser window. While these methods are not completely infallible and can possibly be mimicked on fraudulent sites they are a good indication that security precautions are being taken.

Can you correct personal information?

You should be able to review or correct information that is collected about you. The steps should be outlined in the privacy policy and be both convenient and inexpensive.

Can you 'opt-out'?

Wherever your information may be shared you should have the right to 'opt-out'. In some cases there will be a box that you can click to opt-in or opt-out when entering your information. Watch out for small boxes that are already checked as the default since you are implying you are accepting the offer even if you don't personally check the box.

The privacy policy should also give you directions on how to opt-out if the option isn't given when entering your information.

While this list is not exhaustive it does highlight some of the main features that you should look for in a privacy policy. The other information that should always be listed is a contact name, address and telephone number where you can speak to someone regarding the policy.

Chapter twelve
Children online privacy

Protecting your children's privacy

Protecting your children's privacy is perhaps the most important reason in the world to be familiar with the steps necessary to prevent problems with privacy invasion.

While children are not necessarily targets of identity theft they are overwhelmingly susceptible to becoming targets of more insidious crimes which start with the perpetrator learning the identity of your child.

Understanding how chat rooms and email work can help parents teach children to behave safely online. While there are many programs and procedures you can use to track the activity of your children it is most important to educate them about the dangers of chatting online when you don't know who they are talking to or who is reading what they say.

Take similar precautions when your child has a cell phone or text messaging service.

Online forums and chat rooms

Does your child understand that listing their real name, address, telephone number or information like the school they attend can be potentially dangerous if the wrong person decides to get in contact with them?

Do they realize that although the forum or chat room is SUPPOSED to be for children there are possibly adults pretending to be children in order to take advantage of them?

While you do not want to unduly frighten your children it would be more terrifying if you found out that they had been in contact with a pedophile and they did not know how to tell you about it.

Give them rules. Here are some you may want to discuss with your children:

1)   NEVER give out your name, address, telephone number or picture. NEVER agree to meet someone you met online without your parent's approval.

2)   REMEMBER you are speaking in a public area – other people may read what you write.

3)   REFUSE to enter a private chat room. These rooms are closed off to the public and your child may be lured in by an adult trying to seduce them.

4)   Encourage them to TELL you what goes on. Just as you would monitor who they spend time with after school or what TV programs they watch – you want them to feel comfortable telling you about their online friends.

5)   LIMIT the amount of time they spend online. While talking with friends about sports, fashion or other interests may be fun it is not wholly productive for children to spend hours online chatting. It is also more likely that they will investigate sites or forums that are unsuitable for children. Curiosity may lure them in over their heads.

6)   Have the computer in a PUBLIC area of the home. This will protect your children more than any software program. Check on them occasionally just to see what they are doing.

7)   INFORM them about Spam and other email that looks suspicious. If they are not sure tell them to ask you before opening it.

8)   Tell them never to engage in FLAMING. Flaming is an attack on another person who is posting. It is both emotional and uncontrolled – often due to the power of anonymity that exists online. Children have been bullied by other children from school or elsewhere (called cyberbullying) and it can be devastating. Remind your child to show manners to others and be careful how they respond.

9)   Check the HISTORY of their online surfing if you are concerned. It is good to let your child know that you will occasionally check this out as a protection for them.

10)   Use a POP-UP BLOCKER. Sometimes windows open up that advertise pornography or other disturbing images. Make sure you use a pop-up blocking program to protect yourself and your family from this unwelcome exposure.

Even with the previous suggestions you can further secure your child's online experience by looking for organizations like WiredKids.org – these teams provide safe chat supervision to children and teens at WiredKidz.org and WiredTeens.org.

Not only are these areas supervised (although following the above rules is still necessary) but they teach young ones about safe communication, how to use the Internet and other methods of communications responsibly. They also provide information on cyberbullying, cyberstalking, flaming and more. If your child has been a victim you can use their resources to find the information and support you need to fight back.

Reminder
With the age of advanced communications and technology people can learn new things, meet others and connect in ways never before imagined. It is important to respect the need for diligence to ensure these experiences are positive and worthwhile so that you and your family can enjoy these conveniences without undue risk.

Regardless of if you are protecting your financial information, personal information or your child's identity you need to understand how this information can be abused online, through text messaging and in the real world. Educating yourself is the first step. Passing these rules onto your children will protect them and give you peace of mind.

Incorporating steps to protect yourself and your children is a way of respecting your privacy and theirs. While we cannot combat all crimes we CAN make ourselves and our children less likely targets by always showing respect for our personal information and understanding how new technologies, like the Internet, work.

Chapter thirteen
Cookies policies

Cookies and cookie policies

Have you come across any of the following information in a website while browsing?

We use cookies. Learn more

This website uses cookies
Cookies remember you so we can give you a better service online. By using this website or closing this message, you are agreeing to our Cookies notice

By using this service and related content, you agree to the use of cookies for analytical, personalized content and ads. Learn more.

Below is a typical cookie policy and tips on how to handle cookie policies.

1. Statement of intent

From time to time, you will be asked to submit personal information about yourself (e.g. name and email address etc) in order to receive or use services on our website. Such services include newsletters, competitions, email alerts, live chats, forums and Safetyprecaution.com membership.

By entering your details in the fields requested, you enable Safetyprecaution.com to provide you with the services you select. Whenever you provide such personal information, we will treat that information in accordance with this policy. Our services are designed to give you the information that you want to receive. Safetyprecaution.com will act in accordance with current legislation and aim to meet current Internet best practice.

2. Information on visitors

During the course of any visit to Safetyprecaution.com, the pages you see, along with something called a cookie, are downloaded to your computer (see point 3 for more on this). Most, if not all, websites do this, because cookies allow the website publisher to do useful things like find out whether the computer (and probably its user) has visited the site before. This is done on a repeat visit by checking to see, and finding, the cookie left there on the last visit.

Any information that is supplied by cookies can help us to provide you with a better service and assists us to analyse the profile of our visitors. For example: if on a previous visit you went to, say, the resources pages, then we might find this out from your cookie and highlight resource information on a second visit.

3. What is a cookie?

When you enter a site your computer will automatically be issued with a cookie. Cookies are text files that identify your computer to our server. Cookies in themselves do not identify the individual user, just the computer used. Many sites do this whenever a user visits their site in order to track traffic flows.

Cookies themselves only record those areas of the site that have been visited by the computer in question, and for how long. Users have the opportunity to set their computers to accept all cookies, to notify them when a cookie is issued, or not to receive cookies at any time. The last of these, of course, means that certain personalised services cannot then be provided to that user.

NB: Even if you haven't set your computer to reject cookies you can still browse our site anonymously until such time as you register for Safetyprecaution.com services.

4. Use and storage of your personal information

When you supply any personal information to Safetyprecaution.com (e.g. for competitions, Safetyprecaution.com community services or Safetyprecaution.com membership) we have legal obligations towards you in the way we deal with that data. We must collect the information fairly, that is, we must explain how we will use it (see the notices on particular webpages that let you know why we are requesting the information) and tell you if we want to pass the information on to anyone else. In general, any information you provide to Safetyprecaution.com will only be used within Safetyprecaution.com. It will never be supplied to anyone outside of Safetyprecaution.com without first obtaining your consent, unless we are obliged or permitted by law to disclose it. Also, if you post or send offensive or inappropriate content anywhere on or to Safetyprecaution.com or otherwise engage in any disruptive behaviour on Safety-precaution.com, and Safetyprecaution.com considers such behaviour to be serious and/or repeated, the Safety-precaution.com can use whatever information that is available to it about you to stop such behaviour. This may include informing relevant third parties such as your employer, school or e-mail provider about the content and your behaviour.

We will hold your personal information on our systems for as long as you use the service you have requested, and remove it in the event that the purpose has been met, or, in the case of Safetyprecaution.com membership you no longer wish to continue your registration as a Safetyprecaution.com member. For safety reasons, however, Safetyprecaution.com may store messaging transcript data (including message content, member names, times and dates) arising from the use of Safetyprecaution.com community services for a period of six months. Where personal information is held for people who are not yet registered but have taken part in other Safetyprecaution.com services (eg competitions), that information will be held only as long as necessary to ensure that the service is run smoothly. We will ensure that all personal information supplied is held securely, in accordance with the Data Protection Act.

If you are notified on a Safetyprecaution.com site that your information may be used to allow Safetyprecaution.com to contact you for "service administration purposes", this means that Safetyprecaution.com may contact you for a number of purposes related to the service you have signed up for. For example, we may wish to provide you with password reminders or notify you that the particular service has been suspended for maintenance. We will not contact you for promotional purposes, such as notifying you of improvements to the service or new services on Safetyprecaution.com unless you specifically agree to be contacted for such purposes at the time you submit your information on the site, or at a later time if you sign up specifically to receive such promotional information.

5. Access to your personal information
You have the right to request a copy of the personal information Safetyprecaution.com holds about you and to have any inaccuracies corrected. Please use our helpdesk www. Safetyprecaution.com/helpdesk. There will be an administration cost of £10 for accessing this data.

6. Users 16 and under

If you are aged 16 or under, please get your parent/guardian's permission beforehand whenever you provide personal information to Safetyprecaution.com website. Users without this consent are not allowed to provide us with personal information.

7. How to find and control your cookies
If you're using Internet Explorer 6.0, 7.0, 8.0 or 9.0:
> 1. Choose Tools, then
> 2. Internet Options
> 3. Click the Privacy Tab
> 5. Click on the 'Advanced' button
> 6. Check the 'override automatic cookie handing' box and select Accept, Block or Prompt for action as appropriate.

If you're using Mozilla Firefox:
> 1. Choose Tools, then
> 2. Options
> 3. Privacy
> 5. Cookies
> 6. Set your options as required.

If you're using Opera 8+:
> 1. Choose Tools, then
> 2. Preferences
> 3. Advanced
> 5. Select Cookies
> 6. Select your settings using the available options.

If you're using Safari:
> 1. Choose Safari, then
> 2. Preferences
> 3. Security

4. Select options by Accept Cookies as required.

8. How do you know which of the sites you've visited use cookies?
If you're using Internet Explorer:
    1. Choose Tools, then
    2. Internet Options
    3. Click the General tab
    4. Click Settings
    5. View Files
If you're using Mozilla Firefox:
    1. Choose Tools, then
    2. Options...
    3. Privacy
    4. Cookies
    5. Click the Show Cookies button.
If you're using Opera 8+:
    1. Choose Tools, then
    2. Advanced
    3. Click Cookies.
    If you're using Safari:
    1. Choose Safari, then
    2. Preferences
    3. Security
    4. Click Show Cookies button.

9. How to see your cookie code
Just click on a cookie to open it. You'll see a short string of text and numbers. The numbers are your identification card, which can only be seen by the server that gave you the cookie.

This Privacy Policy governs the manner in which Safetyprecaution.com collects, uses, maintains and discloses information collected from users (each, a "User") of the Safetyprecaution.com website ("Site"). This privacy policy applies to the Site and all products and services offered by Safetyprecaution.com.

Personal identification information

We may collect personal identification information from Users in a variety of ways, including, but not limited to, when Users visit our site, register on the site, place an order, subscribe to the newsletter, respond to a survey, fill out a form, and in connection with other activities, services, features or resources we make available on our Site. Users may be asked for, as appropriate, name, email address. We will collect personal identification information from Users only if they voluntarily submit such information to us. Users can always refuse to supply personally identification information, except that it may prevent them from engaging in certain Site related activities.

Non-personal identification information

We may collect non-personal identification information about Users whenever they interact with our Site. Non-personal identification information may include the browser name, the type of computer and technical information about Users means of connection to our Site, such as the operating system and the Internet service providers utilized and other similar information.

Our Site may use "cookies" to enhance User experience. User's web browser places cookies on their hard drive for record-keeping purposes and sometimes to track information about them. User may choose to set their web browser to refuse cookies, or to alert you when cookies are being sent. If they do so, note that some parts of the Site may not function properly.

How we use collected information

Safetyprecaution.com may collect and use Users personal information for the following purposes:
– To improve customer service
Information you provide helps us respond to your customer service requests and support needs more efficiently.
– To personalize user experience
We may use information in the aggregate to understand how our Users as a group use the services and resources provided on our Site.
– To improve our Site
We may use feedback you provide to improve our products and services.
– To process payments
We may use the information Users provide about themselves when placing an order only to provide service to that order. We do not share this information with outside

parties except to the extent necessary to provide the service.

— To run a promotion, contest, survey or other Site feature

To send Users information they agreed to receive about topics we think will be of interest to them.

— To send periodic emails

We may use the email address to send User information and updates pertaining to their order. It may also be used to respond to their inquiries, questions, and/or other requests. If User decides to opt-in to our mailing list, they will receive emails that may include company news, updates, related product or service information, etc. If at any time the User would like to unsubscribe from receiving future emails, we include detailed unsubscribe instructions at the bottom of each email or User may contact us via our Site.

How we protect your information

We adopt appropriate data collection, storage and processing practices and security measures to protect against unauthorized access, alteration, disclosure or destruction of your personal information, username, password, transaction information and data stored on our Site.

Sharing your personal information
We do not sell, trade, or rent Users personal identification information to others. We may share generic aggregated demographic information not linked to any personal identification information regarding visitors and users with our business partners, trusted affiliates and advertisers for the purposes outlined above.

Google AdSense
Some of the ads may be served by Google. Google's use of the DART cookie enables it to serve ads to Users based on their visit to our Site and other sites on the Internet. DART uses "non-personally identifiable information" and does NOT track personal information about you, such as your name, email address, physical address, etc. You may opt out of the use of the DART cookie by visiting the Google ad and content network privacy policy at http://www.google.com/privacy_ads.html

Compliance with children's online privacy protection act

Protecting the privacy of the very young is especially important. For that reason, we never collect or maintain information at our Site from those we actually know are under 13, and no part of our website is structured to attract anyone under 13.

Changes to this privacy policy
Safetyprecaution.com has the discretion to update this privacy policy at any time. When we do, we will revise the updated date at the bottom of this page. We encourage Users to frequently check this page for any changes to stay informed about how we are helping to protect the personal information we collect. You acknowledge and agree that it is your responsibility to review this privacy policy periodically and become aware of modifications.

Your acceptance of these terms
By using this Site, you signify your acceptance of this policy. If you do not agree to this policy, please do not use our Site. Your continued use of the Site following the posting of changes to this policy will be deemed your acceptance of those changes.

Contacting us
If you have any questions about this Privacy Policy, the practices of this site, or your dealings with this site, please contact us via our helpdesk Safetyprecaution.com/helpdesk.
This document was last updated on November 22, 2016
The following is a typical and useful cookies and privacy tips from Google Chrome:

Choose your privacy settings
You can improve your browsing experience using web services. For example, Chrome can use a web service to automatically offer completions

for search terms or website addresses you type in the address bar.

Most of these settings are turned on by default, but you can choose which you'd like on or off.

Computer android iPhone & iPad

> On your computer, open Chrome.
>
> At the top right, click More ⟩ Settings.
>
> At the bottom, click Advanced.
>
> Under "Privacy and security," change your settings:
>
> Turn off any of the privacy settings you don't want anymore.
>
> To manage how Chrome handles content and permissions for a site, click Content settings.
>
> To delete information from your browsing activity, such as history, cookies, or saved passwords, click Clear browsing data.

Learn about each privacy option from the list below:

Use a web service to help resolve navigation errors: When you can't connect to a webpage, you can get suggestions for other pages like the one you're trying to reach. Chrome sends Google the web address of the page you're trying to reach to offer you suggestions.

Use a prediction service to help complete searches and URLs typed in the address bar: These suggestions are based on related web searches, your browsing history, and popular websites. If your default search engine provides a suggestion service, the browser might send the text you type in the address bar to the search engine.

Use a prediction service to load pages more quickly: Browsers use an IP address to load a webpage. When you visit a webpage, Chrome can look up the IP addresses of all the page's links and load the ones you might navigate to next. If you turn this setting on, websites and any embedded content that are pre-loaded may set and read their own cookies as if you had visited them, even if you don't.

Automatically send some system information and page content to Google to help detect dangerous apps and sites: If you check the box, this info will be sent periodically to let Google know about any threats you encounter. It'll also be sent any time you visit a site that's suspicious. This info helps Chrome get better at blocking bad downloads and detecting malware.

Protect you and your device from dangerous sites: Get an instant alert whenever Chrome sees that the website you're going to could be harmful. When you visit a website, Chrome checks it against a list of websites stored on your computer that are known to be bad. If the website matches anything on the list, your browser sends a partial copy of the address to Google to find out if you're visiting a risky site. Learn more about Safe Browsing protection.

Automatically send usage statistics and crash reports to Google: Help us prioritize the features and improvements we should work on by allowing Chrome to send these usage statistics and crash reports automatically to Google. Learn more about usage statistics and crash reports.

Send a "Do Not Track" request with your browsing traffic: You can include a "Do Not Track" request with your browsing traffic. However, many websites will still collect and use your browsing data to improve security, provide content, services, ads and recommendations on their websites, and generate reporting statistics.

Use a web service to help resolve spelling errors: Use the same spell-checking technology in Chrome as Google Search. Chrome sends the text you typed to Google's servers.

Related topics

Read the finer details of how we treat your information in our Privacy Notice.

If you're using a Chromebook at work or school, your network administrator might apply some of these privacy settings for you, in which case you can't change them yourself. Learn about using a managed Chromebook.

Always look for website privacy and cookie policies. They should answer questions about maintaining accuracy, access, security, and control of personal information collected by the site, how the information will be used, and whether it will be provided to third parties. If you don't see a privacy policy or you can't understand it consider doing business on another site.

There is serious concern that identity theft, and more importantly the fear of it, will stop consumers enjoying the benefits of the online world. But there's no reason why it should; the vast majority of websites have good security and criminals make up a tiny fraction of the online community.

But that doesn't mean we can be complacent. Fraud thrives when people forget what they should be doing and many of these scams are easy to see through. There's no need for paranoia but maintain a watchful eye and if in doubt, check it out.

Just like in person, you can't guarantee protection from identity theft online, but by adhering to these suggestions, you should have little problem surfing with peace of mind.

There are some companies out there making offers to help protect you from identity theft. Are they legitimate?

Chapter Fourteen
Contract protection

Using an outside party for protection

There are a lot of ways you can protect YOURSELF from identity theft, but it sure would be nice if someone else would do it for you. Many financial institutions are offering this protection to their customers, and there are some companies who will help you – but much of the time, protection will be for a fee although Cifas (UK) seems to be doing it almost free.

Most of the identity theft plans being offered by a growing number of financial institutions will reimburse customers for out-of-pocket expenses up to a certain dollar amount and help them through the process of contacting creditors, writing affidavits and filing reports.

Paid plans are usually low-cost – around $3-10 per month and provide a certain amount of coverage up to a specific dollar amount. This is done in the form of an insurance policy against loss from identity theft. For example, one company's identity theft plan costs $10 per month and gives coverage for losses up to $15,000.

They will also give customers a copy of their credit report, monitor the customer's credit at the three major credit report agencies daily and issue a report of any changes or possible problems.

These plans also often offer up access to some consumer education plans to help them clear up any problems and prevent identity theft from occurring.

While this all might sound like a stellar idea, many consumer advocates view these plans with a wary eye. Why?

This insurance runs the risk of giving consumers a false sense of security.

You still need to monitor your credit reports and your bank statements. Debit card problems only show up on bank statements. Not credit reports. If there's a problem in your bank accounts, you will probably need to be the one to find it. These types of plans don't do it for you.

If you do take advantage of one of these programs, make sure they will be checking all three reporting agencies all the time. Often, they will check with the first three the first time then monitor only one or two thereafter

So how will you know if this type of insurance plan is for you? It's a personal decision as to whether or not you think you need it. Just remember that having the plan doesn't guarantee you against identity theft.

The FTC says that most identity theft is done by people who have a legitimate reason to see your personal information like health insurance processors, car rental places, and employers.

It's important to keep in mind that this insurance only covers identity theft involving credit fraud. These policies won't help if someone uses your name when they're getting a traffic ticket or has taken over your identity and owes taxes in your name or worse!

We promised you a chapter on all the contact information you'll need. That's up next!

Important contact information (US)

The three major credit reporting agencies:
Equifax – www.equifax.com
P.O. Box 740250
Atlanta, GA 30374-0250
(800) 525-6285
Experian – www.experien.com
P.O. Box 1017
Allen, TX 75013
(888) EXPERIAN (397-3742)
Fax - (800) 301-7196
Trans Union – www.transunion.com
P.O. Box 6790
Fullerton, CA 92634
(800) 680-7289 (U.S.)
1-800-663-9980 (Canada)
If you have trouble getting a financial institution to help you resolve your banking-related identity theft problems, including problems with bank-issued credit cards, contact the agency that

oversees your bank (see list below). If you're not sure which of these agencies is the right one, call your bank or visit the National Information Center of the Federal Reserve System at www.ffiec.gov/nic/ and click on "Institution Search."

Federal Deposit Insurance Corporation (FDIC) www.fdic.gov The FDIC supervises state-chartered banks that are not members of the Federal Reserve System, and insures deposits at banks and savings and loans. Toll free: 1-800-934-3342

Federal Deposit Insurance Corporation
Division of Compliance and Consumer Affairs
550 17th Street, NW
Washington, DC 20429.

Federal Reserve System (Fed) www.federal-reserve.gov. The Fed supervises state-chartered banks that are members of the Federal Reserve System.
202-452-3693
Division of Consumer and Community Affairs
Mail Stop 801
Federal Reserve Board
Washington, DC 20551

National Credit Union Administration (NCUA) www.ncua.gov
The NCUA charters and supervises federal credit unions and insures deposits at federal credit unions and many state credit unions.
703-518-6360
Compliance Officer
National Credit Union Administration

1775 Duke Street
Alexandria, VA 22314.

Office of the Comptroller of the Currency (OCC)
www.occ.treas.gov
The OCC charters and supervises national banks. If the word "national" appears in the name of a bank, or the initials "N.A." follow its name, the OCC oversees its operations.
Toll-free: 1-800-613-6743 (M-F 9:00 a.m. to 4:00 p.m. CST) fax: 713-336-4301
Customer Assistance Group
1301 McKinney Street
Suite 3710
Houston, TX 77010.

Office of Thrift Supervision (OTS)
www.ots.treas.gov
The OTS is the primary regulator of all federal, and many state-chartered, thrift institutions, including savings banks and savings and loan institutions.
202-906-6000
Office of Thrift Supervision
1700 G Street, NW
Washington, DC 20552

U.S. Securities and Exchange Commission (SEC)
www.sec.gov
The SEC's Office of Investor Education and Assistance serves investors who complain to the SEC about investment fraud or the mishandling of their investments by securities professionals. If you believe that an identity thief has tampered with your securities investments or a brokerage

account, immediately report it to your broker or account manager and to the SEC.
202-942-7040
SEC Office of Investor Education and Assistance
450 Fifth Street, NW
Washington DC, 20549-0213

U.S. Postal Inspection Service (USPIS)
www.usps.gov/websites/depart/inspect
For problem with mail theft that cannot be resolved locally, you can contact the USPIS.
You can locate the USPIS district office nearest you by calling your local post office, checking the Blue Pages of your telephone directory, or visiting
www.usps.gov/websites/depart/inspect.
United States Department of State (USDS)
www.travel.state.gov/passport/passport_1738.html
The department of state will investigate instances of passport fraud. You can also find local field office telephone numbers are listed in the blue pages of your telephone book

Social Security Office of the Inspector General
www.socialsecurity.gov
If you have specific information of SSN misuse that involves the buying or selling of Social Security cards, may be related to terrorist activity, or is designed to obtain Social Security benefits, contact the SSA Office of the Inspector General.
Toll-free: 1-800-269-0271
Fax: 410-597-0118
SSA Fraud Hotline

P.O. Box 17768
Baltimore, MD 21235

U.S. Department of Education www.ed.gov
For student loan fraud, first contact the school or program that opened the student loan to close the loan. Also report it to the U.S. Department of Education.
Toll-free: 1-800-MIS-USED
Office of Inspector General
U.S. Department of Education
400 Maryland Avenue, SW
Washington, DC 20202-1510

Internal Revenue Service www.irs.gov
The IRS is responsible for administering and enforcing tax laws. Identity fraud may occur as it relates directly to your tax records. At the website, type in the IRS key word "Identity Theft" for more information.
If you have an unresolved issue related to identity theft, or you have suffered or are about to suffer a significant hardship as a result of the administration of the tax laws, visit the IRS Taxpayer Advocate Service website
www.irs.gov/advocate/ or call toll-free: 1-877-777-4778.

Federal Trade Commission (FTC) www.ftc.gov
1-877-FTC-HELP (382-4357)
FEDERAL TRADE COMMISSION Headquarters:
600 Pennsylvania Avenue, NW
Washington, DC 20580

Department of Justice (DOJ) www.justice.gov
U.S. Department of Justice
950 Pennsylvania Avenue, NW
Washington, DC 20530-0001

Federal Bureau of Investigation (FBI) www.fbi.gov
U.S. Secret Service (USSS) www.treas.gov/usss
The U.S. Secret Service investigates financial crimes, which may include identity theft. Although the Secret Service generally investigates cases where the dollar loss is substantial, your information may provide evidence of a larger pattern of fraud requiring their involvement. Local field offices are listed in the Blue Pages of your telephone directory.

Conclusion

Identity theft is a crime – a serious one. It is punishable by up to 15 years in prison, a considerable fine, and restitution for the monies stolen.

It can be a very scary crime as well. Identity theft is one of the most insidious forms of white-collar crime. In a traditional fraud scheme, prospective victims are contacted directly by criminals who use lies and deception to persuade the victims to part with their money.

Identity theft, however, requires no direct communication between criminal and victim. Simply doing things that are part of everyday routine -- charging dinner at a restaurant or books at an e-commerce Website, submitting required personal information to employers or government agencies, throwing away catalogs received in the mail, or just having casual contact with people – may give identity thieves enough of an opportunity to get unauthorized access to personal data and commit identity theft.

Moreover, identity theft is not a crime committed for its own sake.

Criminals engage in identity theft to further and facilitate many other types of criminal offenses, including fraud.

The Federal Department of Justice is taking identity theft crime very seriously. They regard identity theft as a serious crime problem that requires a comprehensive and coordinated approach. Because anyone – even people who handle their personal data with great care – can become a victim of identity theft, federal prosecutors throughout the country will continue to make use of the identity theft offense and other criminal statutes, and to work closely with the FTC and other agencies, to combat it effectively.

You CAN protect yourself by taking the steps outlined in this book. The next page will provide you with a form to get together your information. Use this form right now – even if you aren't a victim – and keep it in a safe place. It can be a valuable tool in organizing your personal information in general.

Above all, be proactive when it comes to your information. If you take steps to protect yourself right now, you won't have to worry. You'll gain piece of mind without that new motorcycle you didn't buy or that $5,000 loan you didn't take out!

The following websites were used in researching this book:

www.crimes-of-persuasion.com

www.vnunet.com (fipr. Surveillance and security news archive)

www.privacyrights.org

www.consumer.gov/idtheft

www.idtheftcenter.com

Tables

Nationwide Consumer Reporting Companies - Report Fraud

Consumer Reporting Company	Phone Number	Date Contacted	Contact Person	Comments
Equifax	1-800-525-6285			
Experian	1-888-EXPERIAN (397-3742)			
TransUnion	1-800-680-7289			

Credit Card Issuers and Other Creditors

Include mortgage, car loans, personal loans, and student loans here

Creditor and Account Number	Address and Phone Number	Date Contacted	Contact Person	Comments

Bank Accounts

Bank and Type of Account	Phone Number	Date Contacted	Contact Person	Account Number	Comments

Investments
Stocks, CDs, IRAs,

Bank and Type of Account	Phone Number	Date Contacted	Contact Person	Account Number	Comments

Law Enforcement Authorities - Report Identity Theft

Agency/ Department	Phone Number	Date Contacted	Contact Person	Report Number	Comments

About the author

A.E. Ola is an ex-military officer with a keen interest and training in risk management (University of Lagos, Nigeria), CCTV (LCS, London), Christian Religion (University of Wales TDS, Lampeter. UK) and doorman supervision. His inklings in safety and security manifest in his conviction, research and commitment to preserving lives, limbs and love against sabotage, espionage and subversion both in the real, corporeal and digital world.
He is committed to a series of safety and security key books and trainings.

About the book

Identity theft is increasingly turning to a regular issue of concern as fraudsters discover more and more ways of getting hold of personal information required to steal someone's identity.

Identity theft does not always involve taking someone's personal possessions, but stealing the victim's personal information and then using this in an unauthorized way for their own personal gain. The victim may then be implicated as part of a crime and may find it difficult to prove their innocence.

Methods of identity theft **advance quickly as new mediums,** (for example, web-based social networking) grow rapidly, thereby making it almost impossible to completely prevent identity theft, however it is possible to reduce the likelihood of being a target by taking certain precautions. In this book the writer has explored methods used to steal identity and has prescribed how to prevent it and what actions to take if it eventually happens as well as where to get help and prevent further harm.

www.ingramcontent.com/pod-product-compliance
Lightning Source LLC
LaVergne TN
LVHW022321060326
832902LV00020B/3591